Just Another Adventure

Just Another Adventure

Living with Amyotrophic Lateral Sclerosis (ALS)

By

Marcel LaPerriere

Published by Marcel LaPerriere, 2018
Printed in the United States of America
Distributed by Ingram Spark
ISBN: 978-0-692-14974-4

Book design by Dana G. Anderson

The events and experiences that follow are all true, based on the author's recollection of them. In some situations, names, identities, and other specifics of individuals have been changed in order to protect their privacy.

Dedication

Connie — my wife of 46 years.

Table of Contents

Foreword

"Hello. I'm Marcel LaPerriere and I am the local representative for Pan Abode Cedar Homes. You wanted information on models. Let's get together and talk about building your dream home." With that opening line, my odyssey with Marcel began in 2011. My wife and I had some ten or twelve years before purchased an amazing lot on an amazing island a few minutes remote from Sitka. We always thought we would eventually build a house on site, but the challenges of remoteness from the Sitka road system, the rugged terrain, the massive tangle of trees and overgrowth from the lot not being touched since WW II, no dock and only a poor place to moor, the lack of city power, and the lack of spare time with both our careers and our children in school made for inertia of not doing much besides clearing the land a bit and dreaming a lot for over a decade. My wife and I finally realized that we were not getting younger, time was marching on, and that if we were going to build a home for our retirement, we probably ought to get serious.

Since my youth, growing up on a lake in northern Minnesota, I had dreamt of having an oceanfront cedar home with a prow front with lots of windows. We looked at many books and websites at models from Lindal, Pioneer, and others. I found the Pan Abode site and noted that they had very new and exciting house plans, far beyond the dark cedar "Lincoln Log" kit cabins that had been built in Sitka and as US Forest Service cabins throughout Southeast Alaska. We found a model on the Internet that appealed to us, and I submitted the information form and Marcel got in touch with me within 24 hours. To this day, I still can't believe the pure dumb luck of stumbling onto the site and thus getting Marcel to become such a part of our lives for all the years since. "How did you get him to build your house?" I was asked on more than one occasion. "He's the best."

The worst thing I have ever heard anyone say about Marcel is "he sometimes overbuilds a mite." I think that qualifies as "praising with a faint damn."

We signed the contract to have him build our dream home. It is still the only contract I have ever seen with the word FUN in it, as it was expected that both parties should have some. Indeed, it turned out to be magical fun, a cooperative and exciting project that my wife and I were expected to participate physically in far more than we ever imagined.

The logistics of building remote on an island without power or a dock are daunting, but Marcel was totally up to the task. He was a quartermaster extraordinaire, juggling suppliers, shippers, boats, tides, daylight, weather, and labor crews both in Sitka and on Whale Island.

He was always thinking ahead and gave us our orders of what we needed to do to stay on the timeline, be it deciding on final plans, picking out windows, flooring, water systems, whatever, to get things into the pipeline to be barged from Seattle. I learned early in the process, that whenever Marcel had an opinion, it was based on experience and careful thought. I realized it was best to follow his lead. We were never disappointed.

The kindness and generosity Marcel showed to everyone throughout the project was phenomenal. He frequently had bits of whimsy that he added to the house: tile fish for our shower, a tile whale that he sculpted for our hot tub, a drawing that his wife made. He was always doing something extra, beyond what was ever expected. The dogs eagerly looked forward to his arrival everyday with his gifts of bones and toys. He was always eminently fair and instructive with his work crew, frequently hiring people that others might not, but bringing out the best in them, and always giving second chances (or sometimes more) if deserved.

Building remote means no easy way to do anything. No forklifts, no delivery trucks, no cement trucks, no nothing but muscle power and ingenuity, both of which Marcel had in spades. He was the contractor, but led by example himself as the lead grunt, always doing the heaviest lifting. He was called "Sasquatch" in his younger days and it was obvious that name was fitting for this giant tower of strength. I never suspected that this tower would ever so inexorably be tilted over by ALS.

We were into the project well over a year when Marcel began to complain of hoarseness and garbled speech, which I clearly didn't notice at first. It was a long and frustrating journey over many months for Marcel (and his physicians) to finally reach the correct and unfortunate diagnosis. He was able to complete our home and it indeed was a dream he created for us, beyond our wildest expectations.

Not being content with building what was the perfect home for us, he agreed to an additional project last summer, a whimsical tea house, built into the trees, as a final construction opus. It was a grand project that required the assistance of his son and grandson to complete as ALS continued its progression. It was wonderful to watch the three generations working together, learning together, and knowing how precious and fleeting life can be.

As a small town physician, I have the luxury (sometimes curse) of living with patients in the small town and really getting to know them, their families, and their lives. Some diagnoses can be very bad, and my method of mentally coping with a fatal disease has been, at times, to pretend that it wasn't there. I've been upfront with taking that approach with patients and it has generally worked well for both parties. With ALS, that is just not possible. The Monster, as Marcel calls it, continues its march, stripping strengths, sometimes slowly, sometimes quickly, but inexorably weakening that tower of strength that was Marcel.

I have been so impressed with Marcel's approach to his journey. He has far less anger and far more humor than I think I would have given a similar crappy deal from life's deck of cards. He continues to volunteer his time and expertise as his diminishing body permits. His mind is as sharp as ever.

When I heard Marcel was writing a book about his experiences with ALS and seeing his admirable approach to his disease, I assumed that this would be an inspirational book on how to die well and be content with the world. Thinking about it more, this book is not about how to die, but on how to live! With each indignity that ALS manages to pile onto Marcel, stripping him of physical strength after strength, he is left with the dignity of the human intellect.

L'chaim, Marcel! Your spirit lives on.

Thank you for everything.

Donald R. Lehmann M.D. FACSM

2013 Spring. Marcel working on the Lehmann's house walking on the first floor joists above what will become the garage area in the basement. Penny Lehmann photo.

2014. House and Monet Bridge, but not the gazebo and tea house [see below]Marcel LaPerriere photo.

2017. My wife Connie took this photo last fall right after we finished the tea house to the far left in the photo. This was the last project I did as a contractor.

Introduction

"Falling," I yelled, as I foolishly stepped on loose gravel on the friction slab. As I built up speed sliding down the granite slope, I hoped that the steel piton I'd hammered into the rock twenty feet below me would stop my fall. I felt a sudden jerk and then I heard the ping of the piton being pulled from the rock. I started making mental calculations. One hundred feet of rope and no more pitons between Bill and me. That meant I was going to fall 200 feet. Crap. Was I going to hit the bottom of the cliff, or would I stop just short of the bone-breaking thud? I could hear my pants ripping and soon I could feel the abrasions on my knees, hands and elbows. And, I could see the blood I was leaving on the somewhat smooth granite. I literally bounced over the top of Bill, who was stationed in a natural alcove, and could see the look of horror on his face. He, like me, was surprised by my fall, but unlike me, he was overcome with fear. I was too wrapped up in trying to slow my decent to feel the fear I could clearly see on Bill's face. In retrospect, Bill had a right to be afraid, because in the early '70s we did what are called body belays. He knew it was likely going to hurt him as much as me, and he was right. The rope that was wrapped around his waist came to a stop with me hanging at the end, and it gave him a bad rope burn across his lower back. He arrested my fall just a few feet before I cratered into the base of the cliff. It was a near miracle I escaped with only minor abrasions and no broken bones.

From my teen years and much of my adult life I've participated in extreme sports where death is a reality that's never far away. One wrong move could lead to a fatal fall, an avalanche could sweep me to my death, or I could have drowned when cave diving. I'm not an adrenaline junkie, but I've always been a thrill seeker. To me, a man should live life as an adventure and be a productive member of society. I'm now living with a disease that will kill me, but I still live life as an adventure and I'm still trying to be productive. As my ALS progresses it's not easy to look at the disease as an adventure. And it is certainly an adventure I wouldn't have chosen. However, without ALS I would never have experienced many things and would not have met many incredible people associated with the medical profession.

In the summer of 1986, my wife Connie and I launched a 45 foot (on deck) steel custom-built sailing schooner that we named Terra Nova. We chose the Latin name Terra Nova because it means new land or unexplored land. During the 21 years that we owned and lived on Terra Nova, we visited many remote areas on the inland waters, and off shore from Seattle, through British Columbia, and into Southeast Alaska; places only accessible by water. We also had many planned and some unplanned adventures and experiences that would not have been possible without Terra Nova.

Once we found ourselves motoring through extremely rough seas that were open to the ocean on a very dark and stormy night. The forecast for light to moderate winds was wrong, and we soon found ourselves in monstrous seas that were darned scary, but also fascinating. The conditions were right for some of the most incredibly beautiful phosphorescence that we'd ever seen. As each wave crashed into Terra Nova's half-inch-thick bulletproof windows and over the deck, we found ourselves experiencing something that was equally terrifying and engrossing at the same time. The green glow that highlighted each coming wave gave us time to anticipate the next light show while wondering whether we, or our little boat, could take such a pounding. As the boat climbed the ever-growing waves and then surfed down their backsides, the green light from the phosphorescence seemed to momentarily stick to every protrusion on the boats deck. We hung on to the boat for dear life as each wave hit the boat, but we also knew that we were truly experiencing something that few people get to see.

Connie and I have always been intrigued with polar exploration, another reason we chose the name Terra Nova. The boat that transported British explorer Admiral Robert Scott on his ill-fated 1910 to 1913 Antarctica Expedition was named Terra Nova. Bad planning, bad decision making and some bad luck cost Scott and many of the expedition's members their lives. ALS has now become my new Terra Nova. My adventure with ALS will kill me, just like Scott's Terra Nova expedition did him. Unlike Scott, it wasn't bad planning or bad decisions that has sealed my fate; just bad luck. I'm going to do my best to live up to the words Terra Nova. I'll learn and grow from the unwanted adventure and experience that ALS has given me.

In 1996 a good friend took me to an indoor climbing gym in Seattle. I had so much fun I thought it would be a good idea to build an indoor climbing gym in Ketchikan, Alaska where we were living. Connie has always been the common-sense part of our equation when making major family decisions, but I was too persistent, and, in the end, she agreed that we should build the gym. I should have listened to her initial NO, because the gym was never a big money maker, but it's another life adventure I don't regret. In time we added a full fitness gym, which helped the cash flow, but extended the hours that one of us had to be there. Thus I had many hours behind the front desk without much to do. So, when I wasn't busy, I wrote about some of my life adventures. From 2000 when we sold the gym, I did little writing until ALS forced me to be less physically active and I once again sat down behind the keyboard.

When I posted a few of my ALS essays on Facebook, many friends, family members, and even a couple of doctors, encouraged me to publish my writings. One doctor friend even told me that he thought I could help others living with ALS or their caregivers if I put my ALS adventure into a book format. After that conversation, I decided to get more serious, and this is the result of knuckling down to write about what it's been like for me as my ALS progresses. I say what it's been like for me because ALS treats everyone differently. For some, the journey from onset to death can happen as rapidly as six months, but for others, the journey takes years, and sometimes decades. I'm hoping for decades.

I'm finding writing this book to be therapeutic, but I have a couple of other goals. First, I hope to pass something on to my three grandsons. Possibly more important though, is to help others living with what I often call a Monster. ALS is a monster that will strive to make life more and more challenging – not only for the person with ALS, but everyone associated with that person. The challenge often seems overwhelming and not fair. It can lead to negative things too numerous to list. If this book does nothing else, I hope it gives people a sense of hope and helps make things as positive as it can be for all involved.

Morally I have a problem from profiting from others misfortunes, and even my own. It is my desire to donate any profits from this book to helping others living with ALS. Because ALS is such a rare disease there are a limited number of healthcare facilities equipped to deal with the special needs that ALS presents. In my case, I need to travel by plane or take a three-day ferry ride 900 miles to Seattle for the medical attention I need. It's important for people living with ALS, and any disease, to live close to family and where they want to live. Any money made from this book will go towards travel expenses or other medical needs for people living in rural areas with ALS. I would love to help people live a better life where they want to live. Being with family and living in one's own home extends the quality of life of anyone living with ALS.

A Time Line

Approximate Date	Approximate Age	Symptoms
January 2014	61	Started noticing that my voice would sort of slur or break in the evenings.
August 2014	61 1/2	Connie noticed for the first time that I was slurring my voice.
October 2014	61 3/4	After visiting with our family doctor we were sent to see a neurologist at Virginia Mason. I started confusing words when I talked—simple things like saying bird when I wanted to say seagull.
November 2014	61 3/4	Neurologist suggested that I possibly had Primary Progressive Aphasia. Meanwhile I continued to lose my voice. I entered what I call the drunk phase, because I sounded drunk when I talked.
February 2015	62	Neurologist said she was fairly sure I had Primary Progressive Aphasia.
March 2015	62	Neurologist suggested I might have Spasmodic Dysphonia.
April 2015	62	Neurologist, Dr. Elliot, suggested I be tested for Acromegaly.
June 2015	62 1/2	Acromegaly was confirmed.
July 2015	62 1/2	Met with an endocrinologist because my tongue was growing. She put me on a three times daily injection of a drug called Octreotide.

August 2015	62 1/2	Started the Octreotide injections and they made me very sick. I was sick for the whole month and my voice got weaker and weaker. My tongue started to shrink.
September 2015	62 1/2	Had an infusion of Sandostatin Depot. That, too, made me sick. My tongue continued to shrink back to normal size. My voice continued to fade away.
October 2015	62 3/4	Had surgery to remove the tumor on my pituitary gland.
October 2015	62 3/4	Bad reaction to penicillin caused ethermal multiforme. I ended up in the hospital for a week—four days in critical care.
January 2016	63	Balance was getting bad.
January 2016	63	Voice—totally gone.
February 2016	63	Dr. Elliott suggested that I might have Pseudobulbar Palsy.
February 2016	63	Walking okay but breathing is becoming more and more labored.
July 2017	64 1/2	Balance issues are found to be from a disorder called Semicircular Canal Dehiscence.
Summer 2017	64	Walking became harder and harder. Started using a walker off and on.
Fall 2017	64 3/4	Started having problems with constipation.
February 2018	65	Attended an ALS Clinic. My ankles were very swollen. Ended up in the ER at Virginia Mason and two nights in the hospital.
March 2018	65	Had a PEG feeding tube installed.
March 2018	65	Walking declined to the point that I ended up in a wheelchair.
April 2018	65 1/4	Bedsores start becoming an issue.
May 2018	65 1/4	A mysterious bedsore with broken skin forms right behind my right big toe.
June 2018	65 1/2	13 June: Was measured for and ordered a power wheelchair. It is available in Seattle. 18 June: Purchased a newly converted, slightly used 2017 handicapped-accessible van.

Essays

Past History

1/27/16

As I sit on the plane that is, once again, flying Connie and me to Seattle for more medical care, I can't help but think back on the journey that has taken us here. So many unexpected twists and turns. I can easily track the time, because, coincidentally, many of my problems started around the time Bella, our beagle, became part of our lives.

Our beloved little dog arrived at the Sitka Airport as an 11-week-old puppy on the 16 of April 2014. I remember the date because she was supposed to show up on the 15th, Tax Day. But a problem at the Yakima Airport in the airfreight department delayed her arrival by a day.

On occasional evenings six months prior to Bella's arrival I had been noticing that my voice would, from time to time, break. It was as if I was, once again, going through puberty. At the time I chalked it up to a slight allergy to Alaskan yellow cedar, and I figured it was just a reaction to the cedar sawdust that was then, and still is, part of my daily life. I didn't mention anything to Connie because she was having her own health issues, and at the time, it seemed insignificant to me.

Then in August of 2014, we were off to Italy and France for three weeks to climb on the Via Ferrata we love so much. Just prior to our flight to Europe, Connie flew to Seattle a couple of days to see her pulmonologist, Dr.

Horan at Virginia Mason for a follow up visit. Not by coincidence, Dr. Horan is now my pulmonologist, and I'll be seeing her during this visit. When Connie met me in Seattle, and walked to our Air France flight, she noticed I was talking weird. With a concerned look on her face she said my talking sounded like I'd had a stroke. I assured her I hadn't, but had no idea why my voice was sounding so strange.

That summer we enjoyed our time in Europe immensely, but I also noted my voice was getting worse and worse. At this time I starting to think it was a neurological problem that was causing the malady. And as if to enforce that feeling, I noted I'd often have a hard time figuring out the right words to use. That went away over time, and I now think it was because my brain didn't know how to react to a voice coming from me it didn't recognize. Imagine suddenly talking endlessly, as if you were drunk, but weren't; your brain is going to be confused. No doctor has confirmed this theory, but in time I think my brain just rewired itself to adapt to my ever-changing and disappearing voice.

That's all ancient history now, along with three wrong diagnoses. Finally, they pinpointed the cause as ALS. This is going to sound weird because ALS is such a cruel and debilitating disease. But the first diagnosis, Primary Progressive Aphasia [PPA], would have been the one fate I think would have been worse. I'd also very likely be dead by now, since that disease usually kills its victims in two years.

The second diagnosis, Spasmodic Dysphonia, the disease that Robert Kennedy Jr. has, would have been my preferred disease. Other than talking a bit strangely, people who have it live normal lives. Spasmodic Dysphonia was a hell of a lot better than Primary Progressive Aphasia. PPA not only robs one of the ability to talk or write, it manifests itself into the worst dementia one can experience.

Then there was a shimmering of hope when Dr. Elliot suggested that Acromegaly might be the cause of my voice loss. Dr. Elliot, now my ALS doctor, was right; I might have Acromegaly. Sadly, he was wrong that the Acro was the cause of my voice loss. He was also wrong early on when he ruled out ALS. But, in his defense, ALS must usually progress to a point that there isn't any other disease it could be. I think also Dr. Elliot likes to be darn sure when he dishes out a diagnosis of ALS. Like he has said to me several times, "There is nothing worse than ALS." I think he is overlooking Primary Progressive Aphasia.

As I've mentioned before, I expect ALS will likely kill me. I'm also okay that life will become more and more of a challenge. What I'm not okay with is, as ALS progresses it means I'll depend on more and more help from Connie. Over 44 years ago when she said, "I do," I don't think either one of us ever envisioned an end that would include taking care of a husband with ALS.

Speaking of being dependent on someone, that's why Stephen Hawking has now lived for over 50 years with ALS. I'm not saying this in a demeaning way, because I think very highly of Hawking who has contributed greatly to our understanding of the cosmos. Hawking is basically a brain on life support. And, what a brain. For most of Hawking's life he has had one or more full time healthcare attendants. When he travels, it's my understanding that he travels with up to six people in his medical staff. Obviously, that's not something the average person can afford.

As one of my doctor friends said to me, "No one can be sure what or when their final breath will come." To reinforce that statement, I think back to a man I knew who lived with stage-four lung cancer for over ten years, and during that time he continued to work as a welder and smoked like a chimney. Or, one of our town alcoholics who I frequently see staggering down the street, and who I've never seen sober once in the last 14 years. The point of all of this is, even when we know how we are going to die, life is too short not to do our best to be good people and to love the people we love. Bitterness is the one disease that is self-inflicted and should be avoided at all costs.

Local Hospitals

1/29/16

I'm just a bit miffed at the two Sitka Hospitals again. In preparation for our 8th trip to Seattle's Virginia Mason Hospital, I had a CT scan at SEARHC about six weeks ago. I was told basically everything was okay with my lungs. Thank goodness my Sitka general practitioner, Dr. Hunter, said he felt I should see a pulmonary specialist in Seattle.

Virginia Mason's pulmonologist, Dr. Horan, took a quick look at the CT scan we brought on CD and saw a major blood clot and some smaller ones. She called in a Virginia Mason radiologist, and he said yes, the blood clots stood out like a sore thumb.

I don't think I want to do any more tests at either Sitka hospital, since they seem to screw them up. I had to tell the Sitka Community lab people how to do my latest blood test since I'd had it done correctly at Virginia Mason. The young Sitka lady was busier turning examination gloves into turkey Thanksgiving decorations at the lab than researching how to properly do a time-sensitive blood test—another real confidence booster.

Ferry Trip South

3/9/16

As we cruise down Clarence Straits just north and west of Ketchikan with horizontal rain pelting the ferry windows, I can't help but think of all the years that have passed since we moved to Ketchikan in 1982. Most of the many memories are good ones, and even the bad ones always ended up with good outcomes. I remember all the fun adventures we had in these waters, including many right in the water we are now steaming through.

As I face a future of living with ALS, many of the fun things I used to do, will no longer be possible. ALS has already robbed me of my ability to speak and it's robbing me of balance and coordination. It makes me a bit sad to think of the things I'm going to have to give up, but at the same time, it makes me happy that we did all the things we did; sailing, hiking, caving and scuba diving.

If I had any regrets, it was that I spent too much time dedicated to work, and not enough dedicated to fun adventures. I would advise younger folks, to enjoy life, and don't put too much off thinking you'll do it later. I'm living proof that no one is exempt from health issues that can limit what you want to do. Live life to the fullest, fall in love and respect Mother Earth.

ALS?

3/16/16

Yesterday we got to see Dr. Elliott the ALS specialist at Swedish Hospital in Seattle. And today we spent the morning with the ALS interdisciplinary team at Virginia Mason Hospital. Lots of mixed messages today, but the hopeful news was, Dr. Elliott said he was not ready to say that I have ALS. He did say, "It's still on the table," but he also said, "Anything else would be better than ALS—even cancer;" especially my particular version of ALS. So, he wants to rule out every other possibility before he says 100% sure. Everyone has also told us that only time will tell. I've been extra impressed with how kind, compassionate, understanding and professional everyone we have seen has been.

Road Tripping

3/18/16

I read once that Stephen Hawking thought what made him so smart was being stuck in his body, and not being able to easily communicate. I'll never be even one tenth as smart as Hawking, but I have to say, not being able to easily communicate gives me much more time to think and daydream.

One of the symptoms of ALS is spontaneous laughing, which I'm not doing yet. However, Connie might be wondering, because now, I often do just start laughing. I get to thinking about my grandsons, or something stupid I did in the past. Since I can't tell anyone what I'm thinking, I just start laughing. My oldest grandson, Blake, recently got himself in a bit of a pickle helped by number-two grandson, Nate, and I have to say I've laughed out loud at least 20 times just thinking about it.

I also start laughing at my stupidity. Today I kept hitting the cruise control the wrong way, and it took me a minute to figure out why my truck kept speeding up instead of slowing down. Thinking how I would explain to the cop that pulled me over with hand signals, caused laughter. I think Connie figured I'd lost my marbles, but I was envisioning the hand signals I was going to use to explain all this to the cop. I'm guessing he would not have been amused.

April Fool's Day

4/1/16

Today is April Fool's Day. I wish not being able to talk was all just a big joke that would go away. I think being blind would be easier. Not being able to interact through speech is harder than I ever would have imagined. It's amazing how lonely it can be even when sitting in a room full of people.

No News is Good News

4/26/16

They say no news is good news, and I think that's the case for me today, with a bit of good news thrown in. I saw the ALS specialist and the pulmonologist today, and both say I've improved slightly since they saw me six weeks ago.

The ALS doctor says he's totally baffled. I have many of the symptoms of Progressive Bulbar Palsy (This is what they were 95% sure I had in February), but he is less ready to say that today. Many of my symptoms have lessened, and that shouldn't happen with any kind of ALS. But, he also warned that my body could just be learning to deal with the loss of motor neurons.

The pulmonologist said my breathing has improved in the last six weeks. She also said, when they finally figure out what I have, someone will have to publish a paper on it. I don't think she was joking. She is optimistic enough to start me on physical therapy to strengthen my breathing instead of the normal ALS therapy, focused on maintenance and learning to cope with the decline associated with ALS.

So, we really don't know any more than we did in February. That's the "no news is good news."

In February it looked like I had three months to three years to live. I feel pretty good they don't even want to see me again until the end of August.

Medical Stuff

2/28/17

After a quick trip to Seattle and four medical appointments in one day at three different hospitals, I'm still trying to process what the doctors told me. For one thing my breathing ability, at least as shown by the pulmonary tests, has decreased only slightly in the last year. But that's not accurately being reflected in the test, because in real life, I get much more winded than I did a year ago. The doctors also say it's likely not accurate, because with the loss of muscles around my lips, it's impossible to get a good seal on the instrument that does the measurements. One very encouraging result from that test is that my diaphragm muscle has not weakened and is still working mostly as it should. Even with air leaks around my lips, the test shows that I'm inhaling at 80%, which I'm told is good even for a healthy person of my age.

My ALS doctor now thinks the balance issues and the fact I'm losing my ability to walk are related. This is because the nerves that give feedback to my brain are short circuiting, and my brain is not getting the proper information to accurately process walking or balancing. It's crazy because the brain, over time, recognizes that the information is not accurate, and tries to rewire itself. And as more and more nerves short out, my brain may never catch up with repairs fast enough to improve my walking ability. Only time will tell. But, the good news is, the doctor thinks I'll be able to walk, assisted with a stick, for a long time, because my legs are staying stronger than would normally be expected at this stage of any type of ALS. I think the strength is partly because I stay as active as I can. Many studies show that all neurological disorders benefit from staying active and getting moderate exercise.

It's always a waiting game to see where and how things progress. That's as good as news as can be with ALS.

I need to go back to Seattle for more testing as soon as my dear wife, Connie, can figure out how to, once again, schedule three different appointments in as short of time as possible. That's the disadvantage of living in small town Alaska, but I'd rather die a quick death than live full-time in a busy city.

One other thing of note is that my ALS doctor figures the way my disease is presenting itself, I'm likely in a group of around four people in the entire Northwest who are presenting symptoms the way I am. Since this is my third rare disease in as many years, I wonder why I haven't been buying lottery tickets? That's just how unique my malady is. The doctor told me he thinks about me frequently, because to him I'm one of his most interesting, challenging and unique patients in his career as a neurologist who specializes in ALS. Gosh, what an honor.

Email Answer

3/15/17

"It's just a normal part of the neurodegenerative process of your disease," is not exactly what one wants to read in an email from one's doctor. It's a bit depressing to read "neurodegenerative process," but after a good kick in the rear, I also know that depression is not going to help. So, I'm going to keep doing my best to count blessings and not dwell on negative things.

Today, I reached the milestone of needing a walker, not so much for walking (yet) but to help me stand up when I'm getting out of bed. The day will come when I need it for walking too, but I'm hoping that's a long way off. As Connie said the other day, "We know what the outcome is, we just don't know the timeline."

On the blessing side of things, I have a wonderful wife who helps me greatly, along with a wonderful family. My 11-year-old grandson, Nate, with just a little help from me, built me a boot remover, which helps getting my boots off. Nate demonstrated one of my lucky blessings; my three grandsons.

Life is good!

It's Not Dark Yet

8/12/17

During the documentary film, "It's Not Dark Yet," about an Irish man who faces life living with ALS, I once again thought about how lucky I am. Yes, I have ALS, but unlike so many others it hit me later in life. Most of my adult life I've been healthy, sometimes going years between doctor's visits.

A few months back I was sitting in the waiting room at the Neurological Center in Virginia Mason Hospital in Seattle. As I sat in a window seat that has a great view of the Seattle skyline, and a full view of the waiting room, I observed a well-dressed young man in his late 20s or early 30s being escorted by a nurse back into the waiting room. I could see by the look on his face that he was totally shell shocked by something. The nurse asked him to wait while the very nice and helpful lady in Scheduling set up some appointments for him. I was trying not to stare at him, but every so often I'd look over his way and I soon saw that he was reading a small brochure titled "Living With ALS." It was then that I knew why he looked shell-shocked. I assumed one of the doctors had just given him the bad news. I also couldn't help notice that he was wearing a wedding band. I assumed because of his age that he had likely been married less than five years and would soon be telling his wife and possibly children that he had just been handed a death sentence. I also wondered if he had health insurance, and if he'd be able to keep that insurance after he could no longer work? I knew that in an instant, all his dreams had just been shattered.

Another time, as we walked onto the elevator, an even younger, very friendly, and happy man using a pair of arm-brace crutches, walked in right behind us. Connie asked him which floor he wanted, and like us, he was going to Neurology on the 7th floor. As we rode the elevator he said he was excited because he was soon going to find out where his adventure living with a debilitating disease was going to take him next. We didn't ask what his disease was, but I was impressed with the positive spin he was putting on what most of us would find depressing. Since I'm always notoriously early, I watched as he happily walked down the hall with a nurse to his examination room chatting pleasantries all the way.

Just a couple of weeks ago as we were sitting in the Swedish Hospital Neurology Center waiting room, I saw a young athletic looking woman walk in. I could see by the elastic band around her pant leg that she had ridden her bike to her appointment. When I heard her say in a slightly raspy voice that she had an appointment with Dr. Elliot, who primarily only sees patients with ALS or suspected ALS, I assumed that she was likely in the early stages of Bulbar onset ALS.

I'm lucky. ALS hits all ages of adults, but in my case, it waited until I had raised a son and greeted three grandchildren. The odds are totally stacked against the young people mentioned above. It's unlikely that they will make it to even half my age, let alone see grandchildren. The disease they must live with dictates their lives.

If you're ever feeling sorry for yourself go sit in the waiting rooms of any major hospital in any city. Most especially in the Neurological or the Oncology Centers. You will soon see that there are plenty of people who have it much worse than you do. I learn that lesson every time I go to Seattle, no matter if it's at Virginia Mason, Swedish or the University of Washington Medical Center.

If you haven't seen "It's Not Dark Yet," you should. It will have you crying, but also leave you with a warm feeling of hope.

Pity Party

8/20/17

As some of you know, I'm the lucky guy who won the lottery by having three rare diseases. The two main rare diseases are Acromegaly and a rare form of ALS called Pseudo Bulbar Palsy, or possibly Progressive Bulbar Palsy. Plus, along the way I've also experienced the tastes of two other rare maladies. So, you might ask, "Why do I bring this up?" Well I think it's my way not only of coping with the reality of dealing with these diseases, but also to explain to others why I do what I do. I hope to be truthful in this narrative and confess to some the bad sides, too. But, I also hope that I can be a bit inspirational to some who need that kick in the rear or pat on the shoulder. I also confess that my journey has been made much easier by the woman I've spent the last 45 years madly in love with and of course my extended family.

I'm lucky, too, that I have two good friends whom happen to be nurses. To me just the word "nurse" invokes the feeling of caring and in the case of the two nurses I'm talking about, both have hearts of gold. One of those nurses is my cyber pen pal who lives in a small town in England, and we text back and forth frequently. In her kindness, she often gives me good caring advice, for which I'm forever grateful. The other is a woman I've known since we were little kids. She, like my wife Connie and I, got married young; right out of high school. She is married to my oldest friend who is like a brother to me; we have been friends since we were 3 or 4 years old. Sadly, this friend, like me, has a progressive disease that is taking a sad toll on him. Also, sadly, he has been fighting his battle with his disease much longer than I've been facing my battles. So, it is in some ways hard for me to have any criticism of him, yet I will. I also must preface what I'm about to write by saying his rare disease might cause him much greater physical pain than I've had to put up with. Pain can change a person's personality and make them grumpy. Nonetheless, here is my criticism of my friend: his disease often leaves him bitter, angry and likely depressed. His bitterness and anger spills over onto his wife, which is unfair to her. He still loves her and she him, so I'm sure this also saddens him, as it saddens me when I hurt my wife, the woman I love.

I'm going to back up here a bit and share with you some of the best advice an older wiser friend gave me. Here are his Golden Rules for Happiness.

Rule #1 Have someone to love. Well my friend and I have someone to love, so we both have Rule #1 covered.

Rule #2 Have something to do. Here is where my friend and I both have our down falls. You see, before his unfair disease hit him, my friend was one of those guys who could do anything. I truly mean anything. He excelled at everything he did. And, to a much lesser extent, I think I fit that mold, too. Here is what both of us have a hard time accepting; we can no longer do what we use to do because of our physical limitations. I've learned to admit this, and I'm not sure he has. Hence, his frustration that leads to bitterness and anger. And, bitterness and anger always take people down the road of unhappiness, which of course rubs off on everyone around them.

Rule #3 Have something to look forward to. This sort of overlaps Rule #2. Having something to do is often what we two guys look forward to. But, I think my friend becomes overwhelmed knowing he must greatly reduce his "looking forward to" list. And, I'd guess, like me, he also gets very frustrated knowing that many items on his "looking forward to" list, will never get done. We both know our "looking forward to" list should include maintenance on the things we worked so hard to build. Yes, I understand his frustration there. But, what I have a hard time understanding is why he lets his frustration build to the point that it hurts the very person he loves and has been such an important part of the team that built him into the man he is.

I think over the years my friend blew it by not putting more priority on Rule #3. Like me, he didn't set enough time aside for fun and adventure. It bothers me to no end that I had a fraction of the adventures I intended. But my friend can look back on only a fraction of a fraction of the fun and adventures I've had with my wife. Yes, I have many regrets that we didn't put more on our combined "looking forward to" list, but I also know we had more adventures and fun than most people do. The memories of all the fun we had are like medicine to cure the blues. Memories also build strong bonds with loved ones.

I must do a better job at taking satisfaction from my accomplishments; both on the fun list and the actual making progress list. Also, I must do a better job in giving credit to my wife for all she has put up with and all that she has helped me accomplish. I couldn't have done a quarter of what I did without her. I might be wrong in saying this next part, but I think this is one of my friend's biggest failures. He hasn't hailed his wife for the excellent job she has done being the best partner he could have ever wished for.

One thing I've learned from my friend and others. It doesn't do anyone any good to hold a pity party. And, when that pity party hurts the very ones we love, then we should be ashamed of ourselves.

So, will I ever tell my friend this? Likely not. Not that I shouldn't, but I don't want to lose him as a friend, and I sure don't want to add to his already depressing life of ever declining health. I'm still trying to do my best to accept the fact that it's almost for certain all downhill for both of us. But, for as long as I can, I'm going to keep living by those three rules to happiness, and, be as content as I can, knowing I'm not dragging others down with me.

Speechless

8/22/17

"I can't kiss my wife anymore," is how a friend suggested I start this essay. However, instead of doing a complete rewrite, I've added these catchy words to, hopefully, entice you into reading further.

I'm addicted to podcasts. I'm most especially addicted to listening to the podcast "The Moth," where all sorts of true stories are told by some of the world's best amateur storytellers. I like "The Moth" so much because people who are living the "human story" tell their stories. To me, a real story is much more interesting than a fictional novel. I'd love to be one of the storytellers on "The Moth," which is somewhat ironic, since I can't talk. I would be hard pressed to ever tell a story as well as most of their speakers do, but, if I could talk, this is the story I'd tell "The Moth" listeners.

Like many people, I use to contemplate which would be worse; going blind or going deaf. If I was blind, how could I ever experience the beautiful scenery that nature offers us, or even the beauty of manmade objects like some of the cathedrals in Europe I've been lucky enough to see? I can't imagine what it would be like to never be able to see the beauty of the surroundings in my own backyard here in Alaska, or the beauty of the desert in the American west. But, if I was to go deaf, how could I enjoy the beautiful sound of an aria from a Puccini Opera, or a Brahms melody? I'm glad I never had to make this choice, because it would be impossible to decide which would be harder to bear – losing my vision or my hearing.

One thing I never thought about was losing the ability to talk. And now that I can no longer speak, I sometimes wonder if I'd trade getting my voice back for losing my vision or hearing? Some days, I think I would. That sounds weird, but if you think about it, a person's voice is part of his personality. After all, what is a personality, but one's words and actions? So, on top of the frustration of not being able to talk, I also feel as if I've lost part of who I am. As Connie said the other day, while telling an acquaintance about my condition, "The problem with ALS is, a person, over time, gets locked within his own body." She is totally right, and in thinking about it, I almost wanted to cry.

I was going to tell you about the journey of losing my ability to talk, but I'll just condense it. It was a gradual process that took almost two years. It happened in steps, the first being a voice that would from time to time break, as if I was experiencing puberty all over again. Then there was a phase where my brain didn't understand the feedback it was getting as I talked, so I'd scramble the order of the words as they came from my mouth. Just getting to this point was scary enough, and, at that time, I still had hope I could get my voice back to normal. But then came what I call my drunken phase. To me it sounded as if I was drunk, when I surely wasn't. That was likely the most embarrassing phase, because I'm sure some people thought I was drunk, even at seven in the morning. From there it went downhill through a few more phases until my voice was totally gone.

As I was losing my ability to talk, the frustration would from time to time get the best of me. I'd hit my hand or grunt out a noise that was as close as I could come to cussing. Twice this frustration and anger spilled out to the point that I made Connie cry; something I surely didn't want to do. So, I promised myself that instead of letting frustration get the best of me, I'd laugh and try to look at the funny side of my situation. So far, I've been fairly good at that. Just one other time I brought Connie to tears, and for the third time I felt like a real heel. I do try to limit my frustration. The last thing I want to do is let it build to anger, especially if it hurts others around me.

Here is what is especially hard for me. I've already told you about the frustration, but that pales in comparison to not being able to tell my wife I love her. And, to top that off, the disease has robbed the muscles that control my lips from being able to pucker up, so I can't kiss my wife anymore either. For over 40 years I'd end each day telling Connie how much I loved her, and I'd usually thank her for being the best wife ever. And I'd start the next day by telling her the same. I can no longer do that, and it hurts.

I also greatly miss talking to my three grandsons. When Blake and Nate were younger, I loved it when, sitting on either side of me, they'd listen to my stories of their papa's youth, my youth or some of the adventures that their grandma and I have shared. I think the boys loved it almost as much as I did, because they'd often ask for another story or a repeat. By the time my youngest grandson Dane, or, as we call him, "Lucky," was old enough to want to hear stories, my voice was already fading away. That especially hurts, because I don't feel that I can ever get as close to him as I'd like to.

The other thing I loved doing with my grandsons was teasing them. I loved it when it came time for desert. I'd say, "Blake doesn't want that pumpkin pie, because he doesn't like pie. So, you can give me his piece, too." I loved when the boys would protest, saying, "Yes, we DO want our pie." I'd say to everyone, "They are only saying that because they don't want me to get fat. I'll risk the fat to save them from having to eat something they don't want, so be sure to give me their pie, too." Of course, they would protest, and I'm sure they could tell I was joking. To me, it was just one way I could tell the boys how much I cared for them. So yes, I miss that, and that, too, hurts.

I also hate that I can't say, "Hi, how are you doing?" when we meet people in our daily walks. Last summer I even overheard a stranger say, "He sure wasn't very friendly," when I failed to return a greeting after they had been kind enough to say hello as we passed. Several people we meet often must think I'm the most unfriendly guy in town. Or that I'm totally weird. When they talk to Connie, all I can do to be part of the conversation is give a "thumbs up" or an "O.K."

I do have an app on my cell phone that will talk for me, but next time you're in a social gathering, try texting your part of that conversation. This might work if it's just you and one other person, but if you are in a room full of people, try it; you will understand why I get frustrated. Often, by the time I get what I want to say typed into my phone, the conversation has moved on. In fact, the other day Connie, Zach, Jenn and the boys were talking. After I tried about ten times to say something with my phone, only to have what I was going to say no longer relevant, I left the room. It was easier for me to withdraw into my own world than to try to be part of their world. The same thing happened this past summer when we had houseguests. After a day of trying to be part of the conversation, I found it easier to ignore the talk around me, because I couldn't be part of it. Then to make the frustration even more maddening, my phone app isn't working right. When I upgraded the software on the phone, it disabled part of the app, and now the phone and the app are no longer compatible. I do have a different app that I paid way too much for, but it's a piece of junk that's hard to use. The volume can't be turned up beyond mid-volume, so it's hard to hear, and to top that off, the voice is weird. There are other apps, but the reviews I've read aren't very flattering. I'm holding on for the supposed upgrade for the app that I have, even though they have been promising an upgrade for months. Ugh; the frustration is mind-boggling.

I'm also finding out that not being able to talk has safety ramifications, too. How can I tell one of the boys he is doing something I don't feel is safe? Young Lucky seems to test that every time I'm around him. This last Sunday, for example, he was right on the edge of an icy road, and I wanted to tell him he needed to be careful, because a car could slide on the ice and hit him. Fortunately, after a couple of grunts, I got the attention of other adults that were nearby. They saw the situation and said to Lucky what I had wanted to say. But, even with adults it is sometimes a problem. During the summer of 2014 in France, we were in a car with another couple and a driver. We had asked to be let off at the railway station so we could check the train schedules. For some crazy reason, the driver, instead of pulling over to the curb, let us out in light traffic in the middle of the road. I jumped out, but what Connie couldn't see was, if I let her out, she would be right in the path of an oncoming car. So, I pushed her back. She said in an angry voice, "You need to get out of my way." I couldn't tell her why I wasn't letting her pass, and I'm not sure she ever knew why I was appearing to be so rude. We also had to sell our boat. I didn't want to, but not being able to communicate was again a safety issue. This damn disease also makes it hard for me to breathe, so the boat exhaust that one inevitably must breath when docking was unbearable. And, now, with bad balance and barely being able to walk, the boat was out.

With ALS, I'm lucky in that I can still get around. Most people four years into ALS are confined to a wheelchair or dead. However, when I'm having an extra frustrating day, not being able to talk, I have to wonder if it's all worth it? I'm not suicidal, but I must confess that I did Google physician-assisted suicide. I don't know that I want to live if I get to a point that I'm not mobile or require lots of assistance. I had to laugh, too, because when you Google anything to do with suicide, the first thing that comes up is the toll-free suicide prevention phone number. I could see myself calling the number, and then grunting into the phone. The poor person on the other end would surely think it was a prank call or someone with a serious mental health issue.

Now, besides contemplating what it would be like to be blind or deaf, I contemplate which is worse; being blind, being deaf or being mute. I'll never know, or at least I hope I never experience the loss of my sight or my hearing. Not being able to talk is bad enough.

Circumstantial Evidence

9/9/2017

When it comes to science, or the law, I hate that circumstantial, rather than empirical, evidence is used as a benchmark. Empirical evidence is often not as easy to compile as circumstantial evidence. The hypothesis I'm about to lay out is totally based on circumstantial evidence, albeit in my opinion, fairly strong circumstantial evidence.

I started losing my ability to talk, now over three years ago, and started educating myself on all sorts of medical diagnoses, terminology and other things associated with my medical problems. It took several misdiagnoses and time to come up with what the doctors now think is the proper diagnosis. The first wrong diagnosis was Primary Progressive Aphasia, followed by Spasmodic Dysphonia. Then they stumbled onto the fact that I have a rare disease called Acromegaly, which, on rare occasions causes voice loss. After surgery to remove the tumor growing on my pituitary gland, my voice kept fading away. That is when the diagnosis of ALS was first proposed, and later verified—at least verified as much as one can ever verify a neurological disorder.

Let me build my case.

Military veterans, worldwide, have twice the chance of getting ALS than members of the general population. Why? I've never seen this potential answer in print, so I stress that the following is my opinion. Military veterans are more likely to have had more head trauma, more chemical exposure, and higher levels of stress dished at them than the population in general.

Some studies note a higher percentage of people who have suffered head trauma are diagnosed with Acromegaly and other pituitary gland disorders, indicating that head trauma might be a factor in some of those cases.

I also have a rare disorder called Super Semicircular Dehiscence, which is a fancy way of saying there is a hole in one of the semicircular bones in my ear that shouldn't be there. This pinhead-sized hole causes problems with my balance and apparently has been there for years. As we age and our bones become less dense, so the hole likely got larger. When my body could no longer adjust to the larger hole and its associated effects, my balance became compromised. My research showed one of the suspected causes of this ear bone hole is head trauma.

Still with me?

I have three rare diseases that could have been caused by head trauma. I was once an abused child, where knocks on the head were a common thing. My stepmother took great pleasure beating children and my father used to love hitting me on the head with the wood handle of his carpenter's hammer. I thought it was my fault for not being a master craftsman at the age of 12 or younger. He expected me to have the skills that are developed over years and had little understanding why I didn't have superhuman skills and strength. If I bent a nail when driving it, hit the board when doing finish work, didn't point the mortar on rock work right or a host of any other skills, I was guaranteed a knock on the head. My stepmother just loved beating kids—it was an addiction. Fifty years have passed and I still have occasional nightmares of those beatings. One beating sticks out more than the others—I was awakened in the middle of the night with a sharp hit on the head with a hair brush, pulled out of bed, thrown on the floor and repeatedly kicked in the head and body. I had plenty of head traumas growing up.

Let me take the case a little further. A bit over a year ago my younger sister, Chelly, passed away from complications related to gallbladder cancer, which is a rare form of cancer. My mother also had gallbladder problems, so Chelly might have carried the wrong gene. My older sister, Andree, has a rare disease called Dercums Disease, and has suffered her whole adult life with Meniere's disease. I can't prove that any of my sister's illnesses were caused by child abuse or head trauma, they sure could be.

Multiple studies have shown that children who live through any form of child abuse have problems throughout their lives. Other studies have shown that both mental and physical health problems are much more prevalent in adults that have experienced the trauma of being an abused child. Just like rape or other violent crimes, victims of child abuse often carry an extra burden of guilt—as if the crime was their fault. That guilt can exacerbate the negative effects of the crime committed against them and negative ramifications can be felt for an entire lifetime.

So how is my case based on circumstantial evidence? I have suffered from three rare diseases that have been scientifically linked with head trauma. Am I still suffering the ramifications of child abuse? Probably. Is there enough to convince a court of law? Probably not. Either way, I'll always wonder.

For those of you keeping track, I've experienced five rare diseases. Erythema Multiforme manifested itself when I had a bad reaction to a type of penicillin post transsphenoidal surgery to remove the tumor that caused Acromegaly. The reaction nearly killed me when my blood pressure hit 40/20. Mandibular Tori, bone growth on my jaw, caused by the Acromegaly is the fifth. I'd include all five if I were suing my stepmother in a civil lawsuit for damages caused by her repeated beatings.

I'm okay with my health issues related to rare diseases, but I'll never be okay with any child, anywhere in the world, suffering at the hands of adults.

Pain

9/5/17

When you read through the information on ALS, there is very little information on pain and pain management. Maybe that is because, in many ways, compared to other diseases, ALS has few set-in-stone symptoms and patterns, and they are different for each individual.

For me, other than the frequent charley horses, ALS was fairly pain free. That all started to change three or four months ago when the pain started to intensify. That is an ironic twist in ALS. The nerves that control muscle movement stop working, yet pain, smell and taste nerves keep on. Going back to the literature on ALS, there is mention of muscle cramps, which I now can confirm are a real thing. If you read further, you will see, as muscles waste away, joints start to deform. If you look at people with advanced ALS, you can see the joint deformities. I can tell you, as joints start to deform, it isn't pain free. In fact, I'd say joint pain can be bad to extreme. Yet, as much as I read, I found very little information on this side effect of ALS. Even the doctors can tell me little about it. If you think about it, doesn't it make sense? If a joint is becoming deformed, it's going to hurt. If you talk to people who have suffered joint deformities from arthritis, they will tell you it can hurt like hell.

The muscle cramps and joint pain seem to be worse at night. Sleep can be very elusive. Charley horses hit several times a night, to the point that I must get up to work them out. When I lie back down, my joints often feel like I have them in a vise. Sleep is getting harder and harder to come by. No wonder fatigue is one the major side effects of ALS.

I hope you're not taking this wrong, I'm not looking for sympathy. I'm just stating what has become a reality for me as ALS advances. And, I'm not complaining; again, it's just a report of life as it is for me now. I always know it can be worse and feel fortunate that it isn't.

I'm also fortunate that I have a high pain threshold. As a person who has loved many extreme sports, I'm used to discomfort. Try scuba diving in Alaska all day in the wintertime. Even wearing a dry suit, I can tell you, you're going to experience discomfort. Or try caving in Alaska; crawling through wet, muddy, tight places, or rappelling into a cave submerged in a cold waterfall. You're for sure going to know what discomfort is.

Changing the subject slightly, I recall a caving expedition Connie and I were on many years ago. One of the guys on the expedition found he was not cut out for the extreme conditions of Alaska caves. One day while caving on a remote Southeast Alaska island, he told the leader he was going to stay in camp that day and not join us underground. The leader was okay with that because he knew everyone needed a little break from the hard work of exploring and mapping underground. On the other hand, all expedition members had to carry their own weight and contribute to the group effort. So, the leader told the caver who was going to stay in camp that he had to dig a new latrine, as the old one was getting full. Imagine returning to camp at the end of the long caving day to find no new latrine. When asked why he had loafed around camp all day long and hadn't spent an hour digging a new latrine, he said that digging the latrine would have put him out of his comfort zone. So, that became the joke amongst us cavers. Every time the going started getting a little rough, we'd joke that we were getting out of our comfort zones.

My current pain is not out of my comfort zone, and the ALS journey and adventure continues.

Pathologist

10/15/17

Shortly after loading a couple hundred pounds of climbing gear, two tents, and other camping gear into the back seat of a helicopter, I lifted myself into the front seat, fastened my seatbelt, and we took off for one of the thrilling rides of my life. Doc, the pilot, did a free-fall decent with the helicopter rotors only feet from a 4,000-foot-high rock wall, just seconds before a whiteout would keep him from flying. Then he said to me, "Never let yourself be examined by a pathologist." With a great sense of dark humor, Doc rescued us after several days of heavy snow filled too many crevasses on the Baird Glacier for us to make a safe hiking descent from our camp at the 9,000-foot-high Devil's Thumb, near Petersburg, Alaska. Just minutes before he picked me up at near 7,000 feet, he'd taken Connie and our climbing partner, John, down to the Witches Cauldron glacier, an elevation of around 2,500 feet. There were several fast-moving snow flurries with heavy winds in the area, and he knew his chances of taking them all the way to town before returning to pick me up was very slim. However, he did know he could fly the valley back up the glaciers to retrieve them, and later he did. I might add, as we got close to landing at the Petersburg Airport, Doc got on the radio to his operations office and told the ladies in the office, "Cancel the order for the body bags, they made it out alive after all."

Since ALS always ends in death, and that death is normally caused by respiratory failure, the chances that a pathologist gets to examine me are remote. However, if I can, in any way, help research into a cure for this disease, then by all means, examine away.

A few months ago, my oldest brother Jay asked how I was dealing with knowing I have a terminal disease. The short answer is, I'm okay with it. Over my life span I have participated in many high-risk adventures, and if I was going to put my neck on the line having amazing fun, then I had to be okay with dying. I've had hundreds of fun adventures, with more than my fair share of close calls.

In my early 20s, when I fell 60 feet into a crevasse on Mt. Rainer, I remember thinking I was a goner. As I worked my way from being very stuck and tightly wedged between the ice, to ultimately climbing out, I was singing "I am not afraid of dying and I don't really care," from the Blood Sweat and Tears song, "And When I die." But, I did care. Back then, I had an infant son and a young wife, so I had responsibilities, and dying wouldn't have been a very nice thing to do to them. They became my motivation to get myself out of a very bad situation.

A few years back when I got good and stuck cave diving, I was thinking I was about to drown. I think the only reason I didn't die that day is because I was mad at myself for being stupid enough to get stuck in the first place. Then, in October of 2015 when I had a bad reaction to penicillin, my blood pressure went down to 40/20, and I was told yet again, I had come darn close to death. I heard the nurse tell my wife, "Get out of our way, we are trying to save a dying man's life." My wife, Connie, calmly told the nurse she was missing some vital information that would have a bearing on my survival. Connie persuaded the nurse to calm down, and said that a few days before, I had had a tumor removed from my pituitary gland via transsphenoidal surgery. If the emergency crew did something wrong, I could have a Cerebrospinal fluid leak, and they'd see brain fluid leaking out my nose. Obviously, the nurse calmed down and I lived, or I wouldn't be writing this right now.

So, yes, I'm okay with knowing that ALS will likely kill me; that is, if something else doesn't get me first. No, I'm not happy about having ALS, but that's just the breaks of life. My goal is to try to get the most I can out of life with the time I have left. This might sound weird, but I figure someone must be part of the nasty statistic of those unfortunate enough to have ALS. So, why not me? If I can keep just one person off that ALS list, then in a perverse way, I'm glad. None of us lives forever, and ALS might shorten my time on earth. I've accepted that. I'm not happy about it, but I'm okay with it. I'm even okay with being examined by a pathologist; especially if my body can help with a cure for this dreaded disease.

Google

11/1/17

To quote from Google, "Amyotrophic lateral sclerosis (ALS) is a rare group of neurological diseases that mainly involve the nerve cells (neurons) responsible for controlling voluntary muscle movement. Voluntary muscles produce movements like chewing, walking, breathing and talking. The disease is progressive, meaning the symptoms get worse over time. Currently, there is no cure for ALS and no effective treatment to halt, or reverse, the progression of the disease." I've read these words a thousand times and I've tried to stay optimistic about my outcome living with ALS.

It's now been well over three years since I first started noticing symptoms of what turned out to be ALS. I think back to all the doctors I've seen along my journey, and can hear their words ringing in my ears. Things like "Let's hope it's anything but ALS, because it's the very worst of the degenerative neurological diseases." Or, even, "Being diagnosed with cancer is better than ALS. At least with most cancers you have a chance." And, in February of 2015, "You can expect to live another three months to three years." Those were sobering words.

I'll pause here for a minute to insert this. A couple of months ago, one of my Facebook friends via a private message, more or less told me I should never post anything about my health on Facebook, and even seemed miffed that I did. On the other hand, about a year ago another Facebook friend said I should keep a daily journal of living with ALS, and post frequently. That friend said he figured it would be good therapy for me, and it might help others who would read it. As you can see, I'm striking someplace between my two friends' advice. But, I can tell you, living with ALS, I sure wish there was more I could read, more resources, and more answers to my questions.

As some of you know, on the road to my diagnoses of ALS, a doctor figured out I also have, or had, another rare disease, Acromegaly. One thing I found very helpful was a Facebook support group called Acromegaly Support. When I found that Facebook page, I felt I could ask my new hundreds of friends around the world questions, and had a place I could just vent if I wanted to. I never used the venting aspect of that site, but I asked and answered tons of questions. When I did get the diagnosis of ALS, I looked on Facebook for a site similar to the Acromegaly one. I found several ALS sites, but none like the Acromegaly Support site I so liked. I find the ALS sites on Facebook nearly useless. They tell what ALS is, but none of them offer a way to ask questions of others with ALS or provide a shoulder to cry on. I even emailed the two largest ALS foundations, suggesting that, if they really wanted to help people with ALS, they consider offering these features on their Facebook pages. One answered with a kind response saying it was too much work; the other more or less told me to bug off.

Stories of living with ALS on ALS Facebook sites and elsewhere on the web I've seen are highly edited. While I appreciate them, the authors never fully open up and call it like it is. Every story tends to be "touchy feely," which is good. But all too often I find myself wanting to communicate directly with the others living with ALS. Everyone's story is a bit different, but I think we could benefit from a truthful and open discussion; one like I found on the Acromegaly Support site.

I admire the work that the ALS Association has done raising money for ALS research through events like the Ice Bucket Challenge. But, in my case, the organization isn't helpful. Maybe that's because I don't live in a major city. Here are a couple examples. Shortly after I was diagnosed with ALS, we got a call from the ALS office that represents Alaska. For some strange reason that office is located in Eastern Washington State. In that call, they said they could offer me help, but couldn't offer any ideas on what that help would be. Then they emailed, said they'd be coming to Anchorage, and invited me to attend a meeting there. When I said I wouldn't be attending, they left a message on our phone asking if they could swing by the house and meet with me. Connie left a message on their phone asking if they understood where Sitka is? We told them they would be welcome and we'd house and feed them if they did want to stop. We even allowed that we might even be willing to pay for an airline ticket, if we thought it would be beneficial to my well being. Crazy; they never even called back. Just a couple of months ago they again called and said I should swing by the Anchorage meeting. Connie explained that it would be easier for us to attend a meeting in Seattle than Anchorage. They said that would not be possible, since Seattle was not within our territory. I admire their fund-raising work, but they fall short on their other mission – helping people that are living with ALS.

I have found it interesting to read online how people first suspect something is wrong. One person said he noticed his usually good penmanship was deteriorating, and within the year he could no longer write. Another guy, a long-distance runner, said he tripped at the end of a half marathon, but attributed it to fatigue. He kept tripping and tripping until he could no longer walk. He went on to say he missed his old life, and would give anything to be able to just run one more race. A lady said she was always fatigued and couldn't figure out why. Many others have said the first symptoms they noticed were breathing problems. And, possibly the most unique case came from a man I met and climbed with many years ago. A man who might have been the best ice climber in the world from the 70s though the turn of the century. He said the first symptom he noticed was when he slipped while iceskating. The one common theme for everyone with ALS is there comes a day when they reach a tipping point where they know there is no going back.

I started this by saying that I've tried to stay optimist from the first day I noticed something was wrong with my voice. But, I now know I, too, have reached that tipping point. My progression has been like walking down an irregular set of stairs. I take a step down, then hold steady on the horizontal portion of the step before taking another step down. Sometimes that horizontal section is more like a long landing than a step, and I'll hold steady there for a long time. This time I feel like I've taken a plunge off two, three or maybe even four steps. Just in the last few days I've started losing my ability to walk and my breathing has sunk to a point that it's a real concern. So, now I wonder if my inability to breath will kill me before or after I end up in a wheelchair? My optimism is at long last waning. But, I also know that I could be on a long, or even very long, leveling-off spot. Only time will tell.

One last thing. I have noticed that if I post the word, ALS, on Facebook, I'll get a LIKE, and then a quick response from one of several people that appear to be posting from South America. They offer a miracle cure for ALS if I just email them. No one on any of the ALS sites would confirm my doubts or validate said cure. I'm open minded enough to know that there could be something outside of Western Medicine that could help. I'm 99.9% sure it's a scam. It sickens me that there are people out there who prey on people with disabilities like ALS.

How ya doing?

11/16/17

Lately, several people have asked Connie or myself how I'm doing. Plus, in the last two days, others have encouraged me to write more about dealing with ALS. In fact, a doctor friend gave me some encouragement just this morning. So, it's time to sit down at the computer and do a little writing.

As I've mentioned before the only commonality there is between ALS patients is that it's always downhill, with little to no hope of winning the battle. Other than that, everyone has a unique journey along the way until the end is reached. Just the other day I read about a woman who died within six months of her first symptoms. But, I also recently read about a rock and ice climber that I've admired since I was a teen who is now in his 17th year living with ALS. To me, the important thing is to keep a positive attitude and do what you can to live a full life.

I'm going to highlight the positive first.

A couple of months ago I was having endless joint pain and frequent muscle cramps. I'm happy to report that the pain is much less now. And, so are the painful cramps. Doctors are always asking us patients to rate our pain on a scale of one to 10. A couple of weeks ago I would have said that I was always at about six, with spikes to eight. Today I can say that over the last three or four weeks I've seldom hit even a three. And the endless muscle cramps are now down to one or two a day. Fewer cramps and less pain also means I'm sleeping much better. Obviously, I'm extra happy with that.

THE CONSTANT

For well over a year now I've lost muscle tone that keeps my lips and cheeks away from my teeth. So, for the last year the inside of my cheeks and lips are often a bloody mess from being bitten. The good news is, however, since I no longer have the use of my tongue it never ends up between my teeth.

THE DECLINE

I continue to lose my ability to walk, and climbing stairs or going up hill is getting harder with each passing month. One of our favorite short hikes is the Mosquito Cove Loop Trail; that is now about my limit. Last time we hiked the mile and a half loop it took me an hour and 45 minutes, about three times longer than it used to take.

I found another hiking limit the other day, too. Last Saturday we hiked the Indian River Cross Trail, down Yaw Drive Loop; just over a mile. I basically had to crawl up the high step stairs on the Cross Trail part of the loop, so, I'm guessing that my favorite three-mile hike, Beaver Lake Trail, is now out, as well. That is, unless I want to take all day, with lots of rest stops. But, I'm happy to say I'm still averaging three miles a day of walking and that's not bad for being three years into this journey.

Swallowing keeps getting harder and harder. I'm still eating most things, but I have to take a bite, push it around in my mouth with my finger to chew it, and then I can swallow. With dry foods I must sip some water with each bite to moisten them before I can swallow. Liquids like water are getting nearly impossible to swallow, so keeping hydrated is getting harder and harder. Plus, thin liquids, including saliva make me choke more and more often. I've reached a point where I never go a day without choking one or more times, and that sometimes is scary. I now see why choking to death is one of the common causes of death in ALS patients.

MITIGATION

There are no cures for ALS and most drugs are not very effective. However, there is evidence that keeping weight on by eating a high protein, high fat diet helps. So, I'm doing that as much as I can. Also, vitamin B12 and D seem to help, so I'm taking those daily, too.

The other thing I think that helps is keeping busy. I try to have a project or two going at all times, plus working on the house and daily walks are medicine to me.

THE FUTURE

At the end of February, I look forward to a whole host of medical things. The most significant will be having a feeding tube surgically installed. I'm not looking forward to that, but I'm getting to the point I need it, if for no other reason than to get enough water daily. Along with several other appointments, I'll also see a new ALS Doctor who recently started at Virginia Mason Hospital in Seattle. The ALS doctor I have been seeing, that I very much like is at Swedish Hospital. But, as much as I like him, I don't like Swedish Hospital as much as I like Virginia Mason. At Swedish I feel like I'm just a number, but at Virginia Mason the whole hospital is welcoming, and I would just rather go there. Plus, at Swedish I feel like I'm paying for all the glitz that is ever present. At Virginia Mason it's always clean, but not fancy. At Virginia Mason I feel like I'm paying for the medical care and not a fancy building. It's interesting that the new ALS doctor has an MD and a PHD from a school in China. After practicing medicine in China for a dozen years, she came to the United States and did her neurology internship at Mount Sinai Hospital in New York starting in 2010.

As I continue down this path from time to time, I'll post on Facebook. It's the easiest way to let everyone know what's up.

Happy Thanksgiving to everyone. I'm thankful that I have a good life with a loving family and many good friends.

Walking

11/27/17

A few people have been asking me to share more about what it's like to live with ALS. So, from time to time I'll do that, mostly concentrating on one aspect at a time. This time it's walking.

I mentioned before that I'm losing my ability to walk. To me that's much worse than losing my ability to talk. It's now been nearly two years since I've been able to talk. I could never tell you how frustrating not talking is, but I also must say that I've gotten use to it, and now it's just part of life. But, losing my ability to walk is going to be extra hard and I'll have to fight off depression.

Yesterday I walked the ¼ mile trail down to my son Zach and his family's home. To me one of the magical parts of that walk is that the trail is not built to the same high standard of a public trail. This more primitive trail enhances the experience of walking though some beautiful old growth trees with lots of yellow cedars. This close to the ocean, it's rare to have yellow cedar growing in the numbers that there are on that trail, and I enjoy seeing them. Plus, there are some magical trees like the "Dancing Spruce Tree;" it really does look like it's doing perhaps a dance from some ancient druid ritual.

As I struggled back up the trail, finding each higher than normal step near my limit, I realized today's trip could potentially be my last one down that magical trail. I also thought back to when my grandsons were younger, and

I'd often have to carry them up the trail. Or, how I'd often motivate them on the higher steps by calling the steps the mega-mongo steps. I'd say something like, "Wow, you just climbed up three mega-mongo steps," or "Grandma, what do you want to bet that Blake can't climb all the mega-mongo steps?" Of course, being a kid, Blake would say, "Oh, yes I can!," and he would. Yesterday as I reached the last of the mega-mongo steps, 15-year-old Blake was right behind me, and I wondered if he'd have to help me up them. I made it, but I have to confess I was almost crying out of sadness.

One thing that has surprised me is that going down household stairs and steps in the woods is nearly as hard and sometimes harder than going up. If you think about it each time you step down a big step, you momentarily have all your weight on one leg, and that leg is working twice as hard as normal. I also find that on the downhill, it's harder to keep my balance. After a couple of falls I'm starting to get paranoid of taking a major fall.

As I write this I've just come back from a two-mile walk. I'm still able to do it, but I'm extra slow and it exhausts me. I'd say that pretty much all the time now my legs feel like I'm wearing 10-pound ankle weights. Because of that I shuffle my legs more than lift them.

I've also had to learn to pace myself. If I push too hard and my breathing becomes too rapid, it's like having my wind knocked out. I stop breathing and then after a bit of panicking while I try to get my breathing back in order, I often vomit. This happened while walking with my seven-year-old grandson, Lucky, the other day. He said I didn't look very happy carrying a pitcher of water outside to clean up my vomit from our entrance deck.

I mentioned above about having to fight off depression. Being depressed, bitter or angry doesn't help the situation. And, bitterness and anger makes it hard for everyone around you. So, I've resolved to do all I can to stay happy. Having the ones I love around me helps greatly. I also must admit that our little dog, Bella, helps, too.. I'd recommend having a pet to anyone fighting a disease. Family and pets are 100% better than any drugs, legal or illegal; they are some of the best medicine in the world.

Taking and Giving

12/17/2017

Whether you call it Motor Neuron Disease [MND] or Amyotrophic Lateral Sclerosis [ALS], it is an ugly Monster. And the Monster is only happy when it is taking things from its victims. It isn't satisfied with take, take, take. It also wants to give its victim, and anyone else it can, all the negative energy it can muster up. The Monster seems to take joy out of misery and loves taking and passing out as many negative things as it can.

As a victim of the ALS Monster, I have little choice as it robs from me, but I can refuse to take the negative energy it tries to give me. I must be diligent, because it will try to trick me into accepting its gifts of negative thoughts. The other day it was winning, and I almost gave in several times. The night before, the Monster decided to give me the worst muscle cramping I've had yet, and tried to rob me of my ability to breathe. But my body fought back with an overdose of adrenaline and I fought the Monster off. The next day, after it lost that battle and since I had slept so poorly, it tried to give me another gift I didn't want. As I was getting my breakfast ready and feeding our dog I started to get angry at my wife. Every time I moved she seemed to somehow be in my way. Since walking to me is more of a controlled fall and I can't talk, I got frustrated, and then angry every time I nearly stepped into my wife. I wanted to yell, but of course I couldn't. Then I remembered the weapon of humor that I had found almost two years ago. Instead of getting angry, I decided to laugh, and I soon saw the humor in all our near misses. Besides, what's so bad about bumping into someone I love?

After breakfast that same day as I struggled during my morning walk, wondering if I'd make the one-mile loop on the nearly flat trail, I started getting depressed. Since I was walking so slowly, I started to feel sorry for myself, especially when an elderly lady passed me. I also knew that soon the Monster would win one more battle and it would take away my ability to walk. At home and exhausted, I spent much of the day lying on the couch. Because I was doing nothing, the Monster tried depression on me. I made sure it lost, and told it, "You're not going to give me self-pity or depression. I'm not going to give in easily to you. You're an ugly Monster and I'm going to fight you every step of the way." I meant it and I didn't give in.

As I lay there, I recalled when the ALS Monster took away my ability to talk. That gave me endless frustration and often anger. Three times that frustration and anger led me to take it out on the wonderful woman I'm married to. Once I made her cry, and remembered how bad that had made me feel. That was when I decided I would do my best to fight the Monster. Every time it tried to give me negative thoughts or negative energy, I'd fight back with humor or happiness. At that point I knew the Monster would eventually win the overall war by killing me. I decided to make it work extra hard each and every time it tried to rob something from me or give me any negative energy.

The Christmas gifts I wish I could give to everyone fighting the MND Monster, including their loved ones, and caregivers, is the gift of not letting the Monster win any faster than possible. I'd give them the ability to fight the Monster every time it tries to give negative thoughts or energy—no hate, anger, pity, depression, frustration, or anything else that makes you and the ones around you unhappy.

Proof

12/1/17

I have two quotes that I love. I'll start with Carl Sagan's: "Extraordinary claims take extraordinary proof." If I remember right Sagan was talking about UFO's when he said this, but in my opinion, it applies to all claims. If someone tells me they can cure cancer by drinking a special tea, then I want proof to back that up. Show me the double blind clinical trials that support that claim and I'll believe it. On the other hand, if one person is cured by drinking tea, that is not proof. There likely are other factors involved.

My other favorite quote is one by former head of the US Forest Service, Jack Ward Thomas. He said, "It's more complicated than you think; it's more complicated than you can think." He was talking about the forest ecosystem, but this surely would apply to the human body.

In one of Carl Sagan's books he mathematically analyzes a supposed miracle where a woman frying a tortilla drops to her knees when she sees the face of Jesus in the fried tortilla. People then come from far away to see the face of Jesus in the tortilla, and they all agree that they have witnessed a miracle. But, have they? For one thing who truly knows what Jesus looked like? Then, if you figure that over 100 million tortillas are fried every day, then mathematically the odds are that sooner or later the face of Jesus is going to show up in the tortilla. Just as the face of Santa, the Easter Bunny and even Micky Mouse will eventually show up in the fried tortilla. So, is it a miracle? Of course not.

If you consider that we humans are estimated to have 19,000 to 20,000 genes and then toss in epigenetics, we're much too complicated to define in simple terms. Without a super computer it's going to be darn hard to mathematically calculate the odds of why some people have rare diseases and others don't. Take identical twins. Why does one twin get cancer or a rare disease and the other not? This is where epigenetics comes into play. What turns a gene on or off, and what makes a gene mutate? How do environmental factors play a role in the mutation of a gene or turning on or off? To me this is where Jack Ward Thomas's quote applies.

Almost every time I post something on ALS or Parkinson's disease, people I don't know come out of the woodwork and suggest some "miracle cure." I've also noted this on other's posts about rare diseases. Would I like a "miracle cure" for my rare disease? Of course, I would. However, I'm not going to send someone in South America, Africa, India or even the US, money so they can then send me the "miracle cure" that's highly unlikely to cure all my ills. The mathematical odds are stacked against these "miracle cures." "It's more complicated than you think; it's more complicated than you can think."

I researched one "miracle cure" snake oil salesman after someone put a link to his cures on one of my posts. This guy claims to have the natural cure for: cancer, herpes, arthritis, obesity, muscular dystrophy, lupus, depression and a whole host of other diseases. Now, don't get me wrong. I'm not saying that diet and exercise can't be part of a therapy, or sometimes even part of a cure. However, many of the diseases mentioned above are way too complicated to think there is a simple answer waiting out there. And, upon digging deeper, I see this man is now serving time for fraud. Yet his books on curing everything under the sun are still on sale, both bound and in e-format. What bugs me the most about this guy's claims is, he says both the FDA and the medical establishment are purposely hiding these natural cures for their own profit. Extraordinary claims take extraordinary proof.

Eating

12/9/17

For many people with ALS, eating is one of the hardest daily tasks. So far that has been true for me. Before I started living with ALS, I had almost no idea how important the tongue is when chewing and swallowing. The tongue not only helps bring food into the mouth, but it then helps position food for chewing and then it moves the chewed food to the back of the mouth, putting it into position for swallowing. In my case my tongue has lost almost all movement, so the best I can do is push food forward in my mouth and chew with my front teeth. As I'm sure you know the front teeth are great for biting food, but not so good for chewing.

To add to the challenge, nothing in my throat works properly, so swallowing is difficult. This means to swallow without aspirating food into my lungs, I must tilt my head forward before swallowing. The more liquid the food is, the more diligent I must be about swallowing. If I let my guard down at anytime when swallowing, I choke. Choking causes me to cough, and coughing often forces air into my stomach, which leads to vomiting. Plus, this often also causes me to stop breathing. Not breathing can be a scary experience. And, if food does end up in the lungs, that's a sure invitation for pneumonia. So, I need to be careful.

The feeding tube that I will have surgically installed in March of 2018 will help me get my daily calories, but will not eliminate choking. One of the most frequent ways I choke is when I swallow my own saliva. I'm betting you swallow saliva many times a day without giving it a second thought. I can't do that. Each time I swallow saliva I have to tilt my head forward and carefully swallow. That is why I tend to not sleep on my back, because when I swallow while sleeping, I'll choke if my head is not tilted forward. From experience I can tell you, it's not much fun waking up choking. The other thing about using a feeding tube is it takes away the pleasure of eating. We humans get some of our biggest pleasure from eating and the tastes of foods. So, I'll keep eating via my mouth and will mostly use the feeding tube for water intake and possibly to take medications, since pills are almost impossible to swallow.

Two years ago, I was given a long list of foods I should no longer eat including nuts, chips, rice and leafy greens like lettuce. I've ignored much of what I was told not to eat and have experimented to see what I can get away with. For instance, I can eat nuts if I place each nut individually between my molars to ensure that I chew them well enough to swallow. Chips are mostly out, but surprisingly potato chips can be eaten because they dissolve in the mouth, whereas corn chips don't. Rice is out, and that surprised me. Nothing is harder to eat than rice; it's impossible to chew and swallow without the use of one's tongue. Fortunately, one of my doctor friends reintroduced me to risotto rice, so that kind of rice is back in. Lettuce is out. However, I can eat spinach leaves if they are soft and cut very small. In fact, my wife Connie, even makes me a wickedly good BLT by substituting spinach for the lettuce. She then puts finely chopped toasted bread, tomatoes, spinach, bacon and mayonnaise in a bowl and I eat my BLT with a spoon.

I've mentioned before that maintaining weight and eating a high protein, high fat diet has been proven to extend life in those living with ALS. But, keeping the weight on becomes a real job because eating takes so long. To eat three meals and two or three snacks a day takes me three to four hours. That's also why I spend a lot of time reading the news or cruising the posts of

Facebook. If I'm going to spend that much time eating each day, I'm going to also be online to help pass the time. I can't work on a project while I eat, because eating requires that I use of my fingers to position food for chewing and swallowing. With my fingers being the substitute for my tongue, I go through a ton of napkins. And, I've been known to wash my hands midway through a meal when they get too covered with food and slobber to wash clean with napkins. I now know why one of the speech pathologists told me that some people with my problem eat over a sink.

From the day I was diagnosed with probable ALS, everyone has told me not to lose weight. It's been one of the healthcare providers number one mantras, "Don't lose weight! Don't lose weight!" But, what they didn't tell me, and I only know because I found an interesting article online the other day, is that as muscles waste away, they require more calories to make them work. Talk about adding insult to injury when it comes to getting enough daily calories.

ALS is different for everyone and no two cases are the same. The other day I read about a man who was diagnosed with ALS and in five months he had lost 68 pounds (30.8 kilograms). You can see why that isn't good, and it gives an insight into why some people die so quickly from this terrible disease.

Connie frequently reminds me that my number one job is to eat and keep weight on. This is one time in my life that my sweet tooth and love of ice cream is coming in handy!

Shame

12/13/17

I was saddened, upset and mad when I watched Donald Trump during the presidential campaign mock a disabled reporter. No one asks to be disabled, and no one is exempt from becoming disabled. To ridicule or mock someone less fortunate than you is pure and simply wrong. Granted, some people make poor life choices that lead to disability, but even they don't ask to become disabled and don't deserve to be mocked. There is no shame in being disabled.

On that tune, I wonder why I drew the unlucky straw? Why have I been inflicted with MND/ALS? Was it the cavalier attitude I took when working with toxic chemicals? Or, possibly all the bad welding fumes I breathed over the years? I'll never know, but I encourage my grandsons to wear proper protective clothing and equipment when working around hazardous substances. I warn them not to make the same mistakes I made in my nearly 50 years of work. Do all you can to stack things in your favor when it comes to long-term health.

Now that I have ALS, I will become more and more disabled. Over time, I've realized that I took my health for granted. I think most healthy people do. I've also become more aware of obstacles that make life harder for disabled people. Here's an example. A couple of years ago in our small town, the city redid the parking lot for our Harrigan Centennial Hall. The new concrete curbs were made more appealing to the eye and maybe friendlier to automobile tires, but, are much harder to step off, or onto than a standard curb. I could walk to the area where the curbs are lower, and I often do. But, as I become more and more disabled, will that be possible? Did the designers give a second thought about ease of use in their design or consider that many of the people who walk on the sidewalks above those curbs are elderly? I think not.

As a house builder, I'd often remind my clients that we all age. And as we age, we need simple things, like more light to see. We find it harder to climb steps or even open doors. I always tried to get my clients to look ahead, five, ten, twenty or more years. Only knowing my mother-in-law would be living with us caused me to think about these things when I was healthy and we built our house. She was aging and would likely need assistance so when we built the house, we built a floor that was handicapped-accessible. Boy, am I glad we did, as I will soon need the simple modifications that we made.

There is no shame in becoming disabled and it's wrong to mock someone who is. If you're not disabled, please be considerate of people who are. Sometimes, unknowingly, folks are not as sensitive as they could be. For instance, when I was losing my ability to talk, a friend said I sounded like a Star Wars Wookie. I didn't mind that so much, but when he started repeating my words with a Wookie accent and laughing, that hurt. He didn't mean to be insensitive and I wasn't overly offended by it. I think that this friend just didn't give it proper thought. Just like the engineers who designed the parking lot didn't give proper thought to something as simple as a curb.

As a society it's our duty to be more compassionate for those less fortunate than we are, including being sensitive to the needs of caregivers and those that love someone suffering from a debilitating disease. Caregivers and loved ones are also victims that get wrapped up in our misfortunes. It goes back to things we should have learned before we were five years old: "Treat others as you'd wish to be treated."

Nostalgia

12/15/17

Not long ago I listened to an enlightening podcast on nostalgia. One of the things I found interesting is that psychologists find we humans are often more nostalgic about hard times in our past than good times. When I thought about it, I found this is true for me. If I were to point my finger at one of the most nostalgic times in my past, I'd go back to 1973 when Connie and I were first married, and had an infant son. We were about as poor then as we have ever been, but we were also extra happy. No, I'm not nostalgic about the south Seattle 2nd floor apartment where the view out our window overlooked a decrepit house with a trashed filled back yard, and where an occasional rat could be seen running amongst the kids playing in the yard. Nor the view beyond that house of a freeway on ramp. The nostalgia comes from living a life with someone I love. Even though we were poor, living paycheck to paycheck, with no extra money for even a simple pleasure like an ice cream cone, we were happy to be new parents living an adventure far away from where we had grown up.

I also find it interesting that when anthropologists look at different cultures around the world, the happiest people, if they have enough food and aren't caught in a war zone, are also the poorest people. Some psychologists think this is because the rewards of work are much more obvious than they are in typical Western society. If you're feeding your family from your own garden and the whole family has contributed to that garden, it's much more satisfying than spending your life commuting to a job you might hate and that robs you of family time.

Now, I'm not saying one has to be poor to be happy. However, I think there are lessons to be learned from these ideas. I think there is a deeper message that revolves around building a strong family with values that don't include needing material things. Poor people living in 3rd world counties that depend on their families seem to be happy people without a fancy car or a big screen TV. Sadly, we in the Western world get too wrapped up in "needing" things that we think will bring us happiness, we lose the importance of family ties.

So, what does this have to do with ALS? The simple answer is family and the importance of family. When someone within a family gets sick, the last thing any family member should do is distance themselves, or be bitter about that sickness or malady. Dealing with any degenerative disease is a struggle for everyone, not just the one who is afflicted with the disease. That is why, to me, it's important for everyone to do all they can to limit depression over unfortunate circumstances. Then strive, despite the circumstances, to maintain as much happiness as possible. It's hard to put a positive spin on something as devastating as ALS, but there is nothing to be gained from being negative. And, everything to be gained by being as happy as you can be.

Happiness and a positive attitude are good medicines that make living with any disease a bit easier. All too often I've watched bitterness, greed and other negative traits tear families apart, and that's not good for anyone. A few years ago I started building a house for a wealthy man and his family. Shortly after we started, he was diagnosed with a nasty cancer and was not expected to live. Since he and I had to find a logical stopping place in the project, I got wrapped up in more of his family feuds than I could have ever imagined possible. In the couple of months we remained on the project, bitterness and greed spilled over onto my crew and me and the working morale was as low as it could get. As we worked to reach a spot to quit, we watched bitterness and greed spread like a wildfire within the family and even to their friends.

I'm happy to say the man survived and another contractor finished the house. Even though the pay was good, I wasn't going back to that toxic environment. A few years have now passed, and I can't help but wonder how many wounds from that time continue to fester and will continue to fester in that family's future.

That brings me back to nostalgia. Life over the rest of my years will not be easy for anyone in my family. I don't imagine in the future after I die that my wife will have nostalgic feelings about my ALS, but I hope she can experience some nostalgia over some of the good times we've had since I was diagnosed with ALS.

Two years ago, I lost my ability to speak and ALS often leaves me fatigued. I'm not always the funnest grandpa to be around for my three grandsons, and even though they will watch me go further downhill, I want them to also someday have nostalgic feelings about having a happy childhood. That should be more than enough motivation for me to keep a positive attitude and push negativity as far away as possible. They didn't ask me to get a degenerative disease, so why would I ever want to take it out on them? My goal is to do everything I can to ensure that they, too, can experience nostalgia someday.

Guilt

12/27/17

I think it's more than my Catholic upbringing that has caused me to go through periods of guilt. I could be wrong, but I think we humans often feel guilt, even when we shouldn't. It seems to me that guilt often follows when we first get sick or are diagnosed with a rare disease.

In my case, the journey to a diagnosis of a motor neuron disease took a few twists and turns over more than a year. As my voice started to fade away though various phases, my neurologist first diagnosed me with a probable disease that, believe it or not, is worse than ALS. As she told me that she suspected I had a disease called Primary Progressive Aphasia, she started crying and gave me a hug. PPA is an early onset dementia that robs its victim of all ability to communicate and then leaves them in a vegetative state. To me, that is worse than ALS, because as bad as ALS is, you still can usually think and communicate. Over a few more months PPA was ruled out, but then an MRI and many blood tests confirmed that I have Acromegaly. That diagnosis explained why, over a period of around 40 years, I've had weird growth spurts where my head, hands and feet grew to above what would be expected as a normal size. It was hoped and assumed that Acromegaly might be the cause of my voice loss, because my jaw and tongue had started a growth spurt. A period of guilt started shortly after that diagnosis, and I wondered what I had done to deserve not only the disease, but also, the progressive loss of my voice.

It didn't help that well-meaning people who I think were also wondering why I was suddenly sick and often fatigued started giving me advice on how to fight the disease. They made many suggestions about what they thought I'd done wrong and what I now needed to do. In no particular order this is what I was hearing; I didn't eat right, didn't exercise enough, I worked too hard, was too stressed, shouldn't believe what the doctors were telling me, needed to try alternative medicine, wasn't praying enough, needed to meditate, and the list could go on and on. It also didn't help that during this time I started a drug therapy to shrink my tongue, which by this time, had swollen to twice its normal size. That two-month round of chemotherapy left me sick as a dog, with endless diarrhea and nausea. Feeling that miserable for those two months left me lots of time to dwell on guilt, mostly because I was too sick to do anything else.

It was also around this time that my younger sister, Rochelle (Chelly), found that her rare gallbladder cancer had come back. She had been in remission for just over a year, and the odds of surviving that type of cancer twice, is near zero. Her situation left me emotionally drained and physically sick. Sometimes she and I would text back and forth, often having much deeper conversations than we ever had in person. Two or three months before she passed away she confided in me that she felt guilty. That guilt came from knowing that she'd be leaving behind four beautiful, young grandchildren. She loved those grandkids about as much as any grandmother can love her grandchildren, and to her, the thought of dying before they grew up caused her to have guilty feelings. She was not guilty of anything. So, why do we humans tend to blame ourselves when we get sick? Chelly never asked to get cancer and she didn't ask it to hit her twice. So why did she feel guilty?

I can understand feeling guilty when poor life choices lead to their illness. I think back to a three-plus pack-a-day chain-smoking boss I had in the 80s and 90s. Shortly after he was diagnosed with emphysema, he told me that when he was awake he was never without a cigarette in his mouth for more than five minutes. Can you imagine every waking hour of every day never being away from a cigarette for more than five minutes? He didn't express any guilt, but he did tell me he regretted that he'd ever started smoking in the first place. I'm happy to say after his diagnosis of emphysema, he quit smoking and I was somewhat surprised when I heard in 2014 that he was still alive.

I still feel guilty every time I think of the burden I've placed on my poor wife, Connie. The number one reason for bankruptcy in the US is medical expenses mounting to the point that the debt can't be paid off. I'll feel mighty guilty if my disease is the cause of losing everything we have worked so hard for. The guilt of causing my wife to file bankruptcy would be the deepest guilt that I can imagine.

I no longer have guilt for being unfortunate enough to have ALS or any rare disease, and I hope that anyone else with a rare disease doesn't feel the guilt they shouldn't.

Depression

12/22/17

I seldom get depressed. Having a degenerative neurological disorder is depressing, but depression is not a good place to let one's self go.

Depression is a complex issue and for some, it's debilitating. For many people extreme depression is not easy to shake off, no matter how hard they try. Many factors can lead to depression, from genetics to a chemical imbalance in the brain. With that said, it's hard for me to be too critical of anyone who is depressed. It can be very complex and I'm not an expert.

I'm not saying I never get depressed thinking about where ALS is going to take me, but when I feel depression coming on, I count all the positive things in my life. And, the positive list always outweighs the negative.

Shortly after 9/11/2001, I went to work for a nonprofit group. One of our missions was to work with what the State called "hard to service youth." If they wanted and were suited for it, we were to get them into job training that would lead to jobs in the maritime industry. It was a very challenging job that took me all over the State of Alaska. Most of the kids we dealt with had "issues;" both minor and major infractions with the law. Some kids were soon to be released from Youth Detention Centers, and our goal was to give them options for success. As you can guess, most came from broken or very dysfunctional families. I didn't feel qualified to work with them, because it took training and specialized education I didn't have. Fortunately, the state sent me to several training sessions that greatly helped.

The most memorable and most helpful of those sessions was put on by Russian Orthodox priest, Fr. Michael Oleksa. I had heard Fr. Oleksa speak a few times before this training session, so knew it would be good. And, it was. The one lesson that helped me work with kids as well as myself, personally, was called Building Assets. He said that many studies have shown that kids with positive assets will fare better than kids who are surrounded by negative influences. So, the idea is to not only bring more positive assets into troubled kids lives, but to point out to them that, even if they don't know it, there are most likely some positive things in their lives they are just overlooking. For instance, if you ask a kid if they think Alaska is beautiful, and they answer yes, then you can point out that the beauty of Alaska is an asset. Of course, the most important asset is to replace people who expose them to negative influences with people who expose them to positive influences. The more positive adults in a kid's life, the more assets that kid has, and the more likely they are to replace bad behaviors with good behaviors.

When I start to get depressed, I just need to look at all the assets I have. Instead of focusing on the negative things about my ALS, I think about how lucky I truly am. I have a wonderful wife, a son with an amazing wife, and three beautiful grandsons who I think are a lot of fun. Then, if I add that I live in a comfortable house that my son, my wife and I built with our own hands, the assets can't get much better. And I can't forget our little beagle, Bella, who gives me continuous joy. Also, I have lots of options to keep myself busy; woodworking projects, and even sitting at my computer writing this essay. Those are assets less fortunate people don't have.

I'm no expert on depression, but if you replace negative things in your life with positive assets, even if you are facing a downhill slide from a terrible disease like ALS, you can still be happy. Try to build more and more positive assets and if you do that, there is no better medicine to fight off the blues.

Decisions

12/23/17

Until recently I've always been the kind of person who doesn't hesitate to make decisions, both small and large. I always figured any decision is better than none, and if I made a poor one, I'd just have to rectify it. It has driven me crazy to depend on a decision from someone else when they didn't or couldn't make one.

That said, ALS is now making it hard for me to make both the simple and the more complex decisions. I often tell my wife that I wish I had a crystal ball to see into the future. If I knew where this dreaded disease was going to take me, decisions would be much easier.

In the temperate rain forest of Sitka, Alaska, where the average annual rainfall is over 10 feet, yes you read that right—10 feet a year, the appropriate outdoor footwear is rubber boots. The brand most use is Xtratuf, or as many locals call them, the "Sitka sneaker." It's called that because it's such a prevalent piece of the apparel in our beautiful little town. My Sitka sneakers are worn out, but since I can barely walk, and I have no idea how much longer I'll be walking, do I get a new pair? If I get a new pair and two weeks later I can no longer walk, that seems like a waste of money. But, since Xtratufs have such a good gripping sole and I walk most days, would the decision to buy new boots be what extends my ability to walk?

Another decision I've been struggling with is whether to spend a week in the hospital to have a pinhead-sized hole in one of my semicircular canal bones closed. This fix would improve my balance and help me when I walk. But, do I need to worry about balance if I can't walk? Or, will the hole in that bone get worse to the point that the disorder called Semicircular Canal Dehiscence gets bad enough to cause other annoying complications, like hearing my own heartbeat? I've been told that can drive a person crazy. Also, any surgery, let alone one where they need to move the brain out of the way to access the semicircular canal area of the ear, can have complications. So, do I consider having the surgery or not? My balance is already bad enough that standing is hard. But, is that even a concern, since standing might soon be a thing of the past? I also enjoy the Sitka Summer Music Festival, where live chamber music is played almost daily for the full month. But, the semicircular canal dehiscence is now making it hard to enjoy the music, because the low frequency notes make me feel like I'm riding in a boat on a stormy sea.

I've also put off having a PEG feeding tube surgically installed, even though the medical professionals have been telling me for nearly two years I should have it done. It hasn't been easy, but I've been able to maintain weight and get enough hydration without one. In this case even though I went against medical advice, I think I've made the right decision. March 1st of 2018 is when I'm scheduled for this simple 45-minute PEG installation, but do I need it yet? Even though eating and drinking are becoming harder and harder, I also know there are associated risks with the PEG, like infections. Several doctors tell me it's no big deal and I shouldn't worry about possible infections. But, I keep reading more and more about the PEG site getting infected. I even recently listened to a podcast where a young man who had a brain injury from an automobile accident and was in one of the best hospitals in the US, died from an infection caused by his PEG. So, should I worry about infections or not? Should I put the surgery off until I can no longer keep weight on?

Decisions, decisions, decisions. Oh, if I only had a crystal ball.

Crawling

12/27/17

We've all heard one version or the other of the saying, "living a second childhood." Sometimes it is used to reflect the positive, as in; "They're having so much fun in their retirement, they're experiencing a second childhood." But, more times than not, it's negative; "The dementia has him living a second childhood."

My second childhood started recently. I've found myself crawling more and more. I'm going back to my toddler years. An example is when I'm on the couch and I want to add some wood to the wood stove. I've discovered it's easier to roll off the couch and crawl the few feet to the stove than to walk. Once there, I open the stove, crawl to the woodpile, and crawl back with one piece of wood at a time. If I need to add five or six pieces of wood, I must make five or six trips. When I'm done, I crawl back to the couch or to the stairs where I can grab the balusters to pull myself up onto my feet.

I'm now rebuilding the first-floor bedroom's ensuite bathroom to make it more handicapped-accessable. For anyone who has either watched a finish carpenter, or who has done finish carpentry work, you'll know that a finish carpenter spends about 1/3 of their day on their knees working on things that are waste level or lower. For me now, I lower myself to the floor, do whatever task I need to do, then crawl to something I can grab to lift myself to my feet. As I've been crawling so much, it's dawned on me that I could possibly get around the house easier crawling, than walking. I'll keep walking for now, but I won't feel any shame diving deeper into my toddler years if that's what it takes. If crawling is what I must do to get from point A to point B, then so be it.

I didn't ask to become slowly paralyzed, so I'm not going to have any shame. I'll keep on doing what I must to adapt to my needs.

Ankles

12/29/17

ALS takes small bites out of a person, until it consumes them. For me right now it's my ankles. Both hurt, but the right ankle feels like it's badly sprained. Today, for the first time, I needed to use a stick, even walking in my own house. Until now I only used a stick outside or in unfamiliar buildings. In my own home I could grab walls, the counter, furniture or even my walker. But now, I can no longer walk without the stick or walker. Maybe the ankle will get better if I relax it for a few days? A week ago I started using Baclofen, a new drug for me, and I wonder if that could be relaxing the muscles too much. I'll see the doctor late this afternoon and we will decide if I should drop it or give it a little longer.

Also, working hasn't been good for my ankles. Even though I only spend a few minutes working from a ladder, my ankles always hurt more when I do. This morning, I was up the ladder just two steps maybe four times and never for more than two minutes, but now I can't walk. Ugh! But, my ankles have been getting weaker and weaker, so maybe using a ladder was just the straw that broke the camels back.

I'm trying to make the main floor bathroom more assessable for me, but I might have to pass the job on to my son, Zach, or grandson, Blake. I love working with Blake, and though he doesn't have all the skills he needs, I can type instructions for him on my iPhone. That might be the solution to finishing the job. Unless my ankles get much better, my ladder days are over.

Note: My doctor decided to cut the three-time per day 5mg Baclofen dose to 5mg just before bedtime. That has done the trick. My ankles feel a bit stronger, I'm not so fatigued during the day, and get no muscle cramps until around 5:00 p.m. Even then, the cramps I get are mild ones. Also, Blake helped me finish the bathroom remodel, which I greatly enjoyed.

Attitude

12/30/17

Friends, family and others often compliment me about keeping a positive attitude, even though ALS is slowly robbing my body of bits and pieces. It's not always easy to stay upbeat, but nothing has been gained by negativity. Has anyone's health ever gotten better by being depressed, bitter, unhappy, or any other negativity? The answer is a solid NO. All negativity does is make living with a malady just that much harder. So, is staying positive in some ways a selfish act? In some ways yes, but it's also an act of giving, because it keeps others happier, too.

This is going to sound totally crazy, but I think I'm as happy as I've ever been, even knowing that it's all downhill from here on out. Yes, Happy!

When I got up out of bed last night to use the restroom, slowly making my way there, and then back pushing my walker in the darkness, I thought about how easy it would be to jump off the edge of the abyss of negative thoughts. When I lay back down, I had trouble falling back to sleep. How was I going to make those midnight trips to the restroom and back in a wheelchair? Or, even how was I going to manage in a wheelchair? The endless questions of where ALS will lead me before it likely takes my life can be overwhelming. I fought off the blues by thinking about all the positive things in my life, and all the negative things I no longer have because ALS forced me to retire.

Granted, I'm not living the retirement I had envisioned, or hoped for. But, even with ALS, things could be much worse than they are. We are far from rich, but we have enough money to eat, heat and light our house, and still have enough to spoil our grandsons with a few presents.

I also thought about how most to my adult life I've been the boss at the various jobs I've had, both working for myself and for others. I thought back more than 20 years to a job where I was the acting boss even though another man was being paid to be boss. He had neither the motivations nor, frequently, the skills to do his job, so, the task mostly fell to me to layout and supervise the work of my fellow workers. When I talked to his supervisor about the inequities of this arraignment, he told me they knew Mr. X wasn't qualified for the job, but that he had more seniority than I did. And besides, he said, "If I promote you to foreman, who would do the work?" Talk about a backhanded compliment and a real morale booster. As much as I loved the physical work and the money of that job, I knew I needed to leave, so I did. It didn't seem fair that an unqualified guy got paid more than I did for doing next to nothing, and that was a downer. I had to leave because, happiness was much more important than money.

More often than not in my 45-plus years of work, I was the boss. For the most of those years, I loved laying out and supervising work. I especially loved to mentor younger workers and watch their skills grow. But being boss isn't always fun. Most employees are good, some great, some beyond great, but there are always the few that add unbelievable stress to the job by being jerks. Some lie, some don't have the skills, some make major mistakes, many are drug or alcohol dependent, but they all added a stress level to the supervisor. Since I no longer have that stress, happiness comes much easier.

I also think about my wife, Connie, and the job she did for close to 30 years. She, too, liked her job, until the last dozen years when she worked for a psychopath. I wanted her to quit so badly, I'd often scream at myself for not being more insistent that she leave. I also knew that her salary and benefits were good, and she'd likely not find a job that was even half as good in our small town. When she did retire and leave, I was ecstatic with joy. For months I could have done endless cartwheels over and over. I was happy because I watched stress leave her. Four years on, she still has a good friend who works for this same psychopath. When they get together and her friend tells tales of work, some stress and anger come flooding back to Connie. But with time these stress and anger levels are lower, and they pass much more quickly. That too brings me happiness.

I started by saying that a positive attitude is the most import thing. It helps to stay positive by surrounding yourself with things that bring joy. I've got that nailed. I love my wife and she brings me endless happiness. My extended family is also a major factor in happiness. And, I can never overlook my three grandsons who make me smile every day. The oldest, at 15, makes me proud of most everything he does. Most amazing about him is that at the ripe old age of about 12 he took an interest in blacksmithing. In three short years he has taught himself, and is now on the way to mastering that dying skill. Then there is the middle grandson, who is 11 years old. He not only has kindness flowing from every inch of his body, but he's a walking encyclopedia. When he takes an interest in something, he reads books or does endless online research on the subject. Lately his interests have been drones, planes and submarines. He can tell you anything on those subjects and many, many others. Connie often says, she is surprised by what he retains, and I agree. Then the youngest, at seven, gives us all a big laugh by being the "Encyclopedia of Little Known Facts," as we jokingly call it. Since he was about four, he could weave a yarn about any subject and talk with the authority of an expert, even though 99% of what he said was total fabrication. How can I not be happy?

Bella, our little beagle, Bella, also brings me endless joy. Not only do I laugh at her several times every day, but she seems to have a 6th sense about where I'm experiencing pain at any given time. She either licks the hurting spot or snuggles her warm body against it. Connie's number one rule for getting a puppy 3 ½ years ago was, "There is no way she is sleeping in our bed." The 5th or 6th time that cute little puppy put her front paws up on the bed and cried with those big brown eyes, rule number one went out the window. Today, neither one of us can imagine life without a warm, wiggly snuggly little puppy lying against our bodies each night. Just last night my right shoulder was hurting, and the next thing I knew, there was a living and slightly snoring heating pad snuggled up to the sore spot. Again, how can I not be happy?

I've never made a New Year's Resolution in my life, but if I were to start with 2018, I'd resolve to keep fighting off the blues and any negative thoughts. I'd make that one, because it's one I can easily keep.

Running on Paranoid

1/2/18

I define paranoia via the meaning of a persecution complex. It's an irrational and obsessive feeling or fear that one is the object of collective hostility or ill treatment. In this case the ill treatment is coming from the ALS Monster.

Most of you know what it's like to be driving down a road wondering if you have enough gas to reach the next filling station. Or, maybe you're on a cross country trip and you take the calculated risk that you can pass a town, thinking that you can make it to the next town and fuel source. You take the risk, and as you drive on, paranoia creeps in. You oscillate between watching the fuel gauge and the odometer, and soon you are watching the gauges with more intent than the road or surroundings. You keep making mental calculations; will I make it or not? That's what I mean by running on paranoid.

As ALS progress I find myself running more and more on paranoid. Let's go back to the automobile analogy. When I knew my car was running in top condition, had a working fuel gauge, and was getting, let's say, 30 miles to the gallon, it was easy to calculate how far I could drive without hitting the paranoid phase. However, I now have the same automobile, but I'll be lucky to get 10 miles per gallon, and sometimes maybe only two. Now there's no constant. Will I get ten miles per gallon, or two miles per gallon? Or maybe

I'll get lucky and get 12 miles per gallon today? Without knowing how much gas I'll burn or how far I can drive, that means I'll always be driving close to, or in the paranoid phase.

Here's the ALS equivalent that I experienced today. After not sleeping well last night, this morning I had to decide if I wanted to work on my bathroom remodel project or walk. Thinking I wouldn't have enough energy to do both, I decided to work on my house project. Then, after two morning naps in between short spells of working and lunch, I saw I had enough energy to take an afternoon walk. It's becoming more and more apparent that I'm slowing down each day. Connie and I started walking in the park, and I was moving at the speed of a snail. Still, I felt like I could make the full one-mile loop. Then the equation changed. A couple of hundred yards into the walk, we met a lady that Connie had been meaning to call and wanted to talk to. In days gone by, that would have been a fortuitous occasion, and in some ways, it was today, too. I was forced to stand for 10 to 15 minutes, and, as strange as it might sound, standing takes more energy than walking. By the time we started walking again I was running on paranoid. Could I make the full mile? Or, at least to the first crossover trail to the main trail back to the parking lot? Maybe I could make it to the second crossover trail? When do I turn back or continue to the crossover to the shorter main trail? Will I hit the wall and run out of energy? Then what? Connie can't drag me, and I'd feel stupid calling for a rescue in the park. This is now often my normal day; I'm running on paranoid.

In less than two months I must make a trip to Seattle, and I'm wondering how I'm going to get around? Will I need to take a taxi? What about all the walking in the two hospitals I'll be visiting? Can I do it, or will I need a wheelchair? I'm still weeks away from the Seattle trip and I'm already running on paranoid, which seems to be the new norm. The ALS Monster is messing with my brain and making me paranoid.

Value

1/2/18

In 1968, just a few days before I turned 15, I learned a valuable life lesson: "There is value in all of us." So, how did I learn this lesson? As strange as it might sound, I learned it from an event that was taking place nearly 1,800 miles from where I lived in Denver.

The black and white images on the evening TV news and in the Denver Post newspaper showed that sanitation workers striking in New York City were bringing one of the major cities of the world to its knees. Within three short days the garbage men had a city of close to eight million people starting to drown in their own waste. Within a week the city could no longer function, and the strike was ended. This got me thinking. How can someone that many in society look down upon be so important? The answer, of course, is, there is value in all of us. Even then I wondered if a normal citizen of such a big city would have noticed if the stockbrokers of Wall Street, those we hold in high esteem, had been striking? It's often the people we don't see that have as much and maybe more value than the ones we do see.

Around this time I started to question other things we value. I was living with my aunt and uncle in a totally dysfunctional family that valued possessions and alcohol over love and family. Since I had left an abusive home just the year previously, I already knew what it was to grow up where the only love that could be seen, was the love of material goods. In both the families it had become totally obvious to me that the values where in the wrong place.

Now that I'm living with ALS, it's even more clear to me that family and love are much more important than a new car, new TV or a fancy house. As we watch our son and his wife raise their three boys, the happiness in my grandsons is 10 times what I had as a child. That makes me happy. I'm proud to see that my son and his wife know where real value lies. Putting love and family over material goods and possessions will always be a winning combination.

During the last three years I've spent more than my fair share of time in hospitals and medical clinics. I'm always grateful for the fine care I receive from the doctors, nurses and medical technicians. But, I also always remember to look deep and be thankful for the cleaning staff and those that haul away the garbage. After all, the best doctor in the world would have hard time doing his or her job if they were standing in a garbage heap.

It's much the same in a family. We all need to see value in each other. We all need to do what we can to help ease out the bumps, to make love and understanding flourish over hatred, bitterness and all the other garbage that all too easily accumulates when value in others isn't appreciated.

I'm glad I started learning those lessons young. Over the years I of course, have failed many times by starting down the wrong path. When I do see myself failing, I've tried to look back at the images of the garbage piling up on the streets of New York. When those in charge of NYC didn't see the importance of the garbage men, they overlooked a most valuable life lesson: "There is value in us all."

Driving

1/6/18

ALS robs its victim bit by bit. This time it's robing me of my ability to drive and that means it's robbing me of some independence. ALS also gives something as a keepsake while it robs you. One of its favorite gifts is dependence. As I lose my ability to drive I become dependent on someone else. That's a gift I'd just as soon not receive, but I have no choice in the matter.

I was recently having a hard time deciding if I should buy a new pair of rubber boots called Xtratufs. After several people, both family and friends said, "Buy the boots," I decided to buy them. The store I was planning to get the new boots was closed for the Christmas holiday, and by the date they were open again, I was once again scratching my head. This time, not because I wasn't sure how long I'd be walking, but because ALS gave me something else to add to the equation—ever weakening ankles. Now rubber boots without ankle support seemed like a bad idea. I decided to stick to a hard-soled boot with ankle support when walking outside, and already had a pair.

Switching to the hard-soled boots is causing other issues. The hard-soled boots are not as easy to put on or take off as Xtratufs. What used to take me seconds is now a time-demanding chore. Rubber boots don't need to be laced up and the hard-soled boots do. Normally, lacing boots is not a big deal, but bending over, while sitting makes it hard to breathe, especially since ALS is robing my diaphragm muscle of strength. So, what was once a very simple chore of taking boots on and off is now a five plus minute task. I must rest and take a breathing break between each wrap of the lace and tying the knot. UGH.

I can still drive, but only when wearing short-toped shoes. After I slip in behind the drivers seat, I use my arms to position my leg and I place that leg halfway between the gas pedal and the brake. It is then just a matter of twisting my ankle slightly between the pedals, depending on which function my foot is required to perform. I feel safe driving like that only in our little town with light traffic. The passing of time will soon weaken my legs and ankles even more, and I'll have to stop driving totally.

Yes, the Monster keeps giving and taking. The problem with the give and take is that both are negative things. I am, nonetheless, committed not to accept the bitterness, anger or depression that ALS keeps offering me. I'm standing strong on that, and continue to laugh into the face of the ALS Monster. Laughter, humor and love continue to be the best weapons to slow down the Monster that I hate more each passing day. Yes, hate is a negative emotion, but when it comes to ALS, the hatred of that Monster turns into a positive thing. I hate you ALS. You're a Monster!

Heart Break

1/7/18

ALS, amyotrophic lateral sclerosis, is called Motor Neuron Disease, MND throughout the British Commonwealth countries and the UK. That name for this horrible disease better explains what the disease is.

On an ALS UK-based Facebook site, I recently saw a post that breaks my heart; I can't get it out of my mind. Many of the posts on that site bring tears to my eyes, but his one has hit me extra hard. A 33-year-old Australian woman posted that she was recently diagnosed with MND. She added that, within her family, there had already been five deaths from MND, going back to her grandfather. Current medical science states that heredity is only a factor in about 10% of MND cases worldwide; a statistic I doubt.

On this young woman's Facebook page, I saw a very cute little guy staring into the camera, her 16-month-old son, and wedding photos from a couple of years ago. When MND/ALS hits young people, it is often fast and aggressive. For this young woman and her family's sake, I hope this time it is not.

Young people all have big dreams, and this poor couple's dreams are being ripped apart by a devastating, degenerative neurological disease. I want to yell, "That's not fair!" The world isn't fair, and there are terrible things that no one likes to think about. But, since I have MND/ALS it's easier for me to feel empathy for this young woman and her family. With the 24-hour endless news cycle that streams bad new into our homes, her Facebook page was the saddest thing I've seen in a long while.

Don't get me wrong, I'm not depressed, and I remain as happy as ever. But there was a big bite taken out of that happiness when I saw her post. One of my neurologists told me she thinks we are still 200 years away from curing ALS. I hope she is wrong. I'm also happy it waited to hit me until after my son was grown. My hope is that the woman I have been talking about will beat the odds, and she will get to see her son grow into a fine young man.

Fear

1/8/17

My daughter-in-law, Jenn, asked me how I write stories and these essays. I told her that I sit down and write it as if I was verbally telling a story. Usually, I write a couple of paragraphs and then go back a few times to correct as many mistakes as I can find. This essay is an exception to that formula. I've wanted to write an essay on fear for a while now and I must tell you, for some reason it hasn't been easy. In fact, this is my 3rd attempt.

I'm guessing by now you might be thinking that I'm afraid to face or admit fear? That's not it. I am, for some unknown reason, just having a hard time putting into words what I want to say. I think it might partially be because I don't want to sound as if I'm bragging. Or, have I had too many life experiences where fear was such a big part of the experience, I don't know how to condense them from full book to essay format? Also, how do you separate out perceived fear from real fear? Does it even matter what kind of fear we are talking about, as long as we deal with it? I don't know. I think I'm looking for answers to questions that I might not even know?

Many times, throughout my teenage years, and for all my adult life, some people have called me an adrenalin junkie. I don't think that I am, but I have liked living life on the edge. I liked pushing my brain with fear, while exposing my body to the possibility of real harm.

To me, a true adrenalin junkie is a person who pushes well beyond their training and comfort limits to be sure that their adrenalin levels sky rocket. I have seldom done that. Even when going to extremes, I have mostly stayed well within my training level and didn't trigger the adrenal response of fight or flight.

Sometimes when having fun, an adrenalin rush would come from the totally unexpected, doing something I'd done hundreds of times before. About 20 years ago Connie and I helped crew on a 40-foot sail-racing sloop for a few race seasons. Being the big guy on the crew, my job was to work the foredeck; that's where the most height and strength are needed. On this day we were running down wind under a beautiful large spinnaker in an ever-increasing wind force. It was the skipper/owner's call to lower the large sail. We were about to catch the winning boat and were having so much fun he decided to leave the big sail up longer than he should have. There is something very addictive sailing a boat that is way over powered, and way too fast. In the sailing world it is likened to riding on a runaway freight train because of the speed and power. But, the power and feeling come from tactile senses; like the sound of the water surging past the hull, or the feeling of the wind on one's body. It's a feeling that is hard to describe. But just like a heroin junkie needs the next fix, a racing sailor starts wanting and then needing that same feeling of power coming from the wind. When it came time to do a downwind maneuver called a jibe that day, the skipper decided to wait until we were much too close to land for my comfort. This put us in a, "Must do it right mode." He yelled for the jibe, and our well-oiled team started the process. But all didn't go as planned. As we came about with the wind now on port instead of starboard, we went into what is called a "death-roll," with the overpowered yacht trying to flip itself end for end, in what's called a pitchpole. The next thing I knew, I was about eight feet underwater holding on for dear life to the main stay cable of the yacht. Then, as the boat hesitated and rose back out of the water, I found myself several feet above water, only to once again find myself deep underwater. This happened a few more times until the cockpit crew and the skipper got the situation under control; before we dismasted or did a full-on pitchpole. The fear of being underwater on a yacht that had become a runaway train for those few minutes, or was it only a few seconds, brought on a complete adrenalin rush. What followed was total elation, because I hadn't drowned or even gone overboard. The reality that I wasn't wearing a lifejacket heightened my fear in one of those moments. Had I let go of the stay, the boat would have run me over and I might have drowned.

Another time I was comfortably climbing a Via Ferrate, a series of cables and ladders that often climb straight up total vertical cliffs hundred and sometimes even a thousand or more feet. Heights have seldom bothered me, but as I reached a knife-edge well over a thousand feet above the ground below and looked over the other side at an equal or greater drop, I was hit by fear bordering on total panic. My legs started doing what is called "sewing machine leg," they shake up and down as fast as the needle on a fast sewing machine does. That adrenal rush culminated in an urge to run away from the perceived danger. Running at those heights would have not only been foolish, and could have turned what was truly safe into something truly dangerous. Lucky for me I was climbing faster than our guide, or the rest of the group. Being ahead gave enough time to let me get my fear under control and save me from minor embarrassment. I reminded myself that climbing is often more of a mental exercise than a physical one. Even with the extreme drop offs on either side, if I stayed hooked to the cable, I was likely safer then, than I would have walking down a sidewalk in any city in the world. The perceived danger over weighed my sense of what I knew to be safe in reality.

Some people have a fear of heights to the point of phobia. There is no need to fault them for this. I understand because I have my own phobias. I have an irrational fear of needles. On more than one occasion, just the sight of a needle has caused me to pass out. That's a perceived danger of something that, logically, can't hurt me. Yet I still panic with fear and the adrenalin flows at break neck speed through my veins. Because I have been poked and prodded so many times over the last three years, my fear of needles has diminished slightly. But, my brain's hardwiring is having a hard time reasoning with the reality that I've never been hurt by any needle and the chances that I will ever be.

With ALS a whole new set of fears are surfacing. I now need to figure out what I should and shouldn't fear. I learned long ago, if you break things down into small segments, fear, and intimidation can be lessened. As an analogy I was going to use climbing a cliff, but with ALS descending into a cave might be more appropriate. As a caver, I've hooked to a rope peering over the edge of a vertical cave many times. If I think too hard about all the obstacles, discomfort and hazards that might lie ahead, I would be tempted to just walk in the forest. If I did that, I'd miss the chance for a fun adventure. How deep is the drop I'm about to go over? Will the cave be colder than I'm dressed for? Will it be wet and muddy? How about lose rocks, is there one about to fall from the ceiling and hit me on the head? Or, will the cave just end at the bottom of a short little drop? If fear of the unknown overtook us humans, we'd never explore all the options and our knowledge of what the possibilities are would never be known.

Over the last few years I've built a few custom houses. Some were easy projects and some very challenging. I've been asked, "Isn't it overwhelming and maybe intimidating to build a house? The answer is, "It can be if you don't take it one step at a time." Why worry about the color of the interior walls until you figure out how to build the foundation? In the past I've dealt with fear in the same way, "Don't let the unimportant details get in the way of what needs to be addressed." You climb a 1,000-foot-high cliff the same way. Analyze the overall picture, but focus only on what you need to focus on at the time so you won't be overloaded with irrational fears.

This is where I'm having a hard time with ALS. I find myself fearing and worrying about things that are hopefully further in the future. It's hard to separate real fears from perceived fears. Do, I need to fear the unknown of a wheelchair, or should I just look at it as another adventure? I've been self-reliant my whole life, and the fear of depending on others haunts me; it scares the dickens out of me. I'm not afraid of dying, but I'm afraid of the unknown path that leads to that point. What should I, and what shouldn't I fear? What are the things that I should fear, and what are the things that will trick me into fearing them when there is no need? Am I fearing and worrying about things that I should logically procrastinate into the future? I'm not saying I shouldn't be thinking about what's out there, but just like picking the interior wall color before the foundation is built, some of the fear and worry might be better to postpone.

There is also what I call the 2:00 a.m. fear. That's when I fear where and how fast ALS will take me to the end. It's also when I think the most about death. Again, I'm not afraid of dying, but I do think about the various ways to die. I think about an elderly friend who wanted to die from a heart attack in his sleep. He said that would be the easiest way to go. And, he did just that. After mowing his small lawn, he sat in his easy chair to take a nap and never woke up. I think we'd all like to die that way. Knowing that death in ALS patients is often prolonged scares me, too. To use an old saying, it scares me to death; I'll skip that. Oh, if it was only that easy.

Circling back to unexpected fear and the inevitable adrenaline, ALS gives me both one or more times daily. During each day I will, from time to time, choke, usually on my own saliva. If I'm concentrating too deeply on something, I forget to tip my head forward when I swallow and then I choke. Sometimes I choke so badly, I'm on the edge of passing out and I start to panic. To me, choking triggers real fear.

My wife's totally irrational fear of bears nearly crippled her desire to hike and explore the woods. In Alaska we often fight our fear of bears by making jokes about bear attacks. We joke that to survive a bear attack you only have to outrun your hiking partner. As we head into the woods we sometimes joke that we are wearing better running footwear than our partners. Connie and I walk most days within the National Park that sits right inside our town boundaries. Brown bears, including some of the biggest in the world, are frequently seen within the park and they fish for salmon. During the summer of 2017 there were bear sightings in the park almost every day for over two months. From now on when we hike in the park, it will be comforting for Connie to know she no longer has to fear the bears. She can easily outrun me.

I'm not an adrenalin junkie, but I do love a good adventure. It's not always easy, but I'm trying to look at living with ALS as just another adventure. I need to crawl deeper into the cave to see what's around the next corner, and I need to do it with a smile on my face. Just like I'm not going to let depression, bitterness or anger run my life, I'm not going to give into fear. Fear can be as crippling and negative as any emotion. I'm not going there. I'm going to keep holding my head high and face the fears head on.

Love

1/10/18

It wouldn't take a psychiatrist or anyone else who studies the brain to understand why, as an adult, I hated hugs or showing the emotion of love to anyone but my wife. One of my regrets is that I didn't work harder to overcome this disability. However, I also know that mental wounds are slow to heal, and you're lucky if they heal at all.

One of the things I'm most proud of is that my older sister, Andree, my younger sister, Chelly, and I broke the circle of violence. We didn't become child abusers as our father and our stepmother were. Mental wounds are often the hardest to mend. But, the three of us did overcome the physical and mental abuse that, many unfortunate children don't. My hat's off to my sisters, because they out performed me, not only becoming better parents than I was, but also being able to openly show affection to their children and others.

As an adult, I think the thing that would make me shrivel into submission and want to cower in a corner more than anything was a hug by another adult. Especially if that hug was initiated by a female other than my wife. Psychoanalyzing myself, I think that's because my stepmother liked to put on a show in public where she'd hug us as if she loved us. But out of the public eye, her mental illness took over. The joy she took from beating, belittling and, in my case even sexually abusing, nullified any affection she showed in public.

And I think the only love our father experienced from us was having a source of free labor. He motivated us to be his slaves, mostly though verbal abuse, but he, to a lesser extent than his second wife, also seemed to get some joy out of abusing us physically. In psychoanalyzing him, I'd say he had an inferiority complex with his peers, and to make himself feel equal to them, he had to put on a show. Over time, to get the dopamine stimulant high he craved, the show became more and more of a need to him. Often in public settings, he too would pretend to love his children while singing mostly Irish ballads in front of a crowd. Yes, that Frenchman sang Irish ballads; he had a great Irish tenor voice and he sang the ballads well. But, his public display of love for his children was just as much a performance as his singing. Out of the public eye, as he would lift me off my off my feet by pulling on my ear. He'd yell, "You're worthless, you're a total piece of shit, you will never amount to anything," and on and on.

So, what does this have to do with ALS? For one, I think living in those conditions as a child may be helping me cope with the disease as I near the end of life. Bookends of adversity on either side of a great life full of happiness. Some studies of holocaust survivors and others who have survived horrible conditions, show they are often more resilient to future adversity. But, more important to me, it shows love and positive attitudes can overcome the worst things that life can toss our way.

In my case the love I have had for my wife and my family, even though I didn't show it openly, has helped me heal many of my childhood wounds. And the love from my older brother who saved us from the hell that our father and stepmother put us though has also helped me heal. Further, love and family will help me as ALS continues to progress.

Do I wish I had been better at showing affection? Yes, especially now that I can no longer speak. I also wish I would have been better at accepting hugs from family and friends. I'm still working on that, but I'm guessing the old mental wounds are just too deep, and that I can never overcome the feeling of near panic when someone approaches me for a hug. I've gotten better, but I still have a long way to go.

In our culture and many cultures around the world for a man to show affection is a sign of weakness. To me, that's sad.

As Diana Ross sang:

What the World needs now, is love sweet love
It's the only thing that there's just too little of
What the world needs now is love, sweet love,
No not just for some but for everyone.

What a beautiful thought, expressed though a beautiful song. When living with a progressive disease like ALS, this is especially true, not just for the one suffering from the disease, but for everyone.

Physical Therapy

1/11/18

If you look online at various ALS sites, it's hard to get a consensus. Are strength exercises a good thing or a bad thing for ALS patients? As near as I can tell all the old data suggest that trying to strengthen muscles is a bad thing. This is because one needs to break a muscle down before making it stronger. A non-technical explanation of muscle building is, during a workout the muscle fibers are damaged, and as the muscle repairs itself, it gets stronger. More recent data suggest that mild exercise is likely good for muscles that are wasting away because of ALS. That is if you don't overdo it. I agree with the latter. But how do you know how far to push before doing damage that isn't going to be easily repaired?

A couple of different doctors have told me that they think walking is the best physical therapy I can do. I liked that advice, because I like walking and I've never been much into formal exercise. To set time aside to go to the gym has always seemed a bit strange to me. If you do physical work, you achieve two things at the same time. I'd much rather be climbing up and down ladders, packing lumber, or splitting and stacking firewood than going to the gym. To me those kinds of exercise are "win-win's." You get the exercise the body needs while also doing something productive.

With that said, I recently started going to physical therapy, and I agree with my physical therapist that light exercise will be good for me. What surprised me was peddling just five minutes on a stationary recumbent bike's easiest setting kicked my butt, and made my calves and other leg muscles sore. This was a big eye opener as to how far downhill I've slipped.

Last night I was reading online about ALS while I was trying to ignore my sore leg muscles, and I needed to use the restroom. On the walk back to the computer, just as I walked though a door, my left knee buckled. I fell forward, but caught myself on the doorframe. I once dislocated my right knee, so I knew how painful it is. That's what my left knee felt like. I fully expected to see my left leg sticking out at a 45-degree angle as I had once seen my right leg do when I dislocated it. To put it mildly, I was in pain to the extreme. I grabbed the handrail on our 2nd floor inside balcony and made it back to the computer, wanting to scream in agony. But, I can't scream, so I had to just bear it while I rubbed my leg from the knee down. Fortunately, my wife, Connie, had just come home, and she fetched my walker for me. Since I can no longer swallow pills, I had to chew a couple of aspirins to ease the pain. Here's a little tip for you. If you must ever chew aspirin, chew them with an antacid to help hide the gross taste, and then chase with sips of water.

Now the question is, was the little bit of bike riding the cause of the knee giving way, or was it just a coincidence? Or, could it be that an hour before the knee gave way I took a muscle relaxant called Baclofen that helps with nightly muscle cramps? I'll keep going to PT, and keep taking the Baclofen and I'll see how it goes.

As the saying goes, "Getting old isn't for wimps," and neither is ALS.

What's in a Name?

1/15/18

Like most boys growing up in the 60s I had a big stack of baseball cards. We boys took our baseball cards as seriously as money, and in fact, our cards sometimes were our currency of choice. On the playground conversations like this could be heard, "I'll give you a Mickey Mantle and a Hank Aaron if you do my homework for me." This would spark a round of hardcore bargaining, and if lucky we'd sucker someone into doing our homework without have to sacrifice our best cards. Just like real money, different names on the cards had different values. For instance, even though a Babe Ruth card was common, it had a higher value than, let's say, a Billy Martin card, one not very common. Since Martin wasn't known as a big star in the baseball world his card had little value to us. As we unwrapped our bubble gum, I still remember being excited to see if our penny investment had paid big dividends by giving us a valuable card or just a mediocre card. We always hoped for another Babe Ruth or maybe a Sandy Koufax—both valuable cards.

Another valuable card, one that represented a legendary man for more than baseball, was a Lou Gehrig card. At the age of eight, we had no idea what a neurological disease was, but we knew that Lou Gehrig was so famous that he even had a disease named after him. We knew, too, that this once famous ballplayer died from the disease that was named after him, and even to a young boy, that was mighty cool. Though Mr. Gehrig had been dead for over 20 years, how he bravely faced death was the legend that made his card extra special and valuable.

It's been almost 60 years since baseball cards were a part of my life, and now that I have Lou Gehrig's disease, or Amyotrophic Lateral Sclerosis (ALS), I feel like lobbying to have his named disassociated with the horrible disease. I can't think of anything worse thing than naming a fatal disease after any person, let alone someone who had already become famous by being great at his chosen profession.

Take Parkinson's disease. I'd hate to think that it would become called "Michael J. Fox" disease. A great honor, however, would be to name a cure after Michael J. Fox, since he has turned his affliction and his fame to raising millions of dollars for Parkinson's research and has helped raise awareness of other rare diseases.

Or look at Christopher Reeve and his wife Dana. They turned Christopher's terrible accident into something positive when they started the Christopher and Dana Reeve Foundation to help people who are paralyzed. I think both Reeve and Fox deserve credit for making something positive out of their misfortunes.

I also think we can learn lessons from these movie stars. It's highly unlikely that any of us that aren't stars will ever raise the kind of money that they have. But that doesn't mean we shouldn't give what we can, both in money and effort, to raise awareness for our disease. Michael J. Fox and, Christopher Reeve are both legends for turning adversity into something positive. Whereas, we will likely never reach the achievements that they did, we can still become legends within our circles of family and friends by turning our misfortunes into something positive. I keep giving what money I can to various good causes and I'll volunteer my time where I can to make the world a better place. In other words, I'm not going to crawl into a hole and give up. I'm going to contribute to society as long as I can.

Now, let's dive a little deeper into the name—Amyotrophic Lateral Sclerosis (ALS). I hate the name almost as much as I hate the disease. But, I also must admit that it makes sense if you break the name down. Amyotrophic means the atrophy of muscles. Lateral means movement from side to side, and Sclerosis means abnormal hardening of body tissue. I prefer the British name, Motor Neuron Disease (MND), because, to me, it better describes the disease. Motor Neuron is a nerve cell that forms the communication pathway from the brain along the spinal cord to the muscles. Whether you call it ALS or MND, the disease causes muscles to waste away because motor neurons are dying, which breaks the communication pathway from the brain to the muscles. The more motor neurons that die, the more muscle loss there is. And, the faster they die, the faster the disease progresses. So, those of us that are living with MND/ALS do our best to slow down the rate at which the motor neurons die, and we do our best to keep as many motor neurons alive as we can.

As humans, we all want to leave a legacy, a tiny bit of immortality. My goal is to make sure my name is associated with as many productive and positive things as I can. I don't want my name tied to a dreaded disease like poor Lou Gehrig's name has been. Though I'll never achieve it, but I strive to be more like Michael J. Fox, who I admire not for his acting, but for what he has done after Parkinson's disease turned his world upside down.

Merchants of Misery

1/18/18

This morning I was listening to a podcast about the proliferation of for-profit substance abuse and rehabilitation clinics across America. The rapid growth of these facilities has been spurred on by two factors. 1. Under the George W. Bush Administration insurance regulations changed to require insurance companies to pay for rehabilitation, and, 2. The opioid crisis. Both have been good for shareholders of the for-profit clinics. To me, these clinics are merchants of misery. The podcast told of a few deaths at these clinics because they put profit ahead of patient care.

Another merchant of misery in the opioid crisis is the pharmaceutical industry that manufactures the opioids. These pharmaceutical companies and their shareholders have made millions, if not billions off the manufacturing of opioids. In 2013 a Drug Enforcement Administration (DEA) agent questioned what he saw as total abuse of regulations, and he suggested that the DEA crack down on the pharmaceutical companies distributing opioids. Sadly, pressure coming from the companies that make the opioid pills shut him down. Every time Congress has tried to put stiffer regulations on the sale and distribution of opioids the pharmaceutical lobby has quashed its efforts. The over prescribing of opioids has been good for the bottom line of the pharmaceutical companies, or as I call them, the merchants of misery.

Let's think deeper. What about the ever-escalating cost of healthcare in the US? When you look at every aspect of healthcare from insurance companies to the pharmaceutical companies and the hospitals, you can't help but ask, who profits from others' misfortunes? The extraordinarily high salaries of pharmaceutical company CEO's and others in upper management of healthcare are paid by you and me. And with the profits of these companies, is it any wonder that healthcare prices continue to outpace inflation?

Think back to the 2017 EpiPen pricing scandal. In 2007 the price of an EpiPen was $57.00 and today it's over $600.00. Mylan, the manufacturer of the EpiPen paid their CEO a salary of 19 million dollars in 2016, and the revenue of the company for that year was 3.3 billion, up 31% from the previous year. This is one of the best examples of putting profits over the well being of people. Mylan epitomizes what I'm calling the merchants of misery.

What does this have to do with ALS? The cost of medical care for ALS patients can be staggering. One example is the drug Radicava, which has shown limited success in treating ALS. By rare disease standards its cost is a bargain at $1,000.00 a month. But, even more staggering is, in the advanced stages of ALS healthcare costs can skyrocket to over $200,000.00 a year. I haven't hit those dollar amounts yet, and I hope I never do. But a 30- to 45-minute visit with my neurologist ALS specialist costs $1,300.00.

The two hospitals that I visit in Seattle are nonprofit hospitals. Why are the cost are as high as they are? When I look at the cost of running the physical plant and all the for-profit companies the medical industry depends on, I have a better understanding.

The cost of the opioid crisis to every citizen in the US is going to be astronomical. Besides the costs of controlling the opioid crisis, what percentage of medical care costs can be attributed to the merchants of misery? To me, a few are getting very wealthy at our expense. If we are ever going to get escalating healthcare costs under control, we need to reign in the merchants of misery.

Second Anniversary

1/19/18

This is one anniversary that I don't feel like celebrating. It's now been over two years since I've been able to talk. I'm sure a person who goes blind gets used to it, and being blind becomes the new norm, just like not talking has become the new norm for me. But, just because it's normal, doesn't mean I don't miss talking. And, it doesn't mean I like it.

I miss saying, "I love you" to my wife. I miss the conversations we had at dinner or when we'd go on long hikes. I miss holding hands and walking in the park as we talked about this and that. I especially miss the conversations we had about our grandsons. And I, for sure, miss talking to my three grandsons. I miss when the boys sat on either side of me and I'd tell them stories of when their papa was young. I also miss not being able to tease them.

My wife Connie has always been a master of the pun. I used to try to match her wit when the occasion presented itself. I still occasionally type a pun into my phone, but it's not the same as saying it out loud. The phone app also can't respond quickly enough if I see something I want to point out. By the time I type in "Hey – look at that the swans that about to land on the lake," it's too late. Or, when I'm riding in the car, while Connie drives, it would be crazy for me to type in a warning about a danger that she might miss.

It's also a bit weird not being able to say "Hi" as I pass someone when we are walking. Even though it's been over two years since I've been able to exchange pleasantries when I pass people, I still wonder if they think I'm a total snob. Other than the fact that I walk with a stick at the speed of a snail, there is nothing to suggest that I have a speech handicap, so I still wonder what others think. Not being able to smile easily makes these encounters even more awkward. I can see why people might think I'm a totally unfriendly snob.

Talking is also how we humans express our personality to others. Not being able to talk is just one more way ALS has robbed a bit of who I am. As the bulbar onset ALS progresses, my face is becoming more and more deformed. The left side of my face now droops and my lips have become expressionless, suggesting bitterness or anger. In fact, Connie said some time ago that I always look angry. I'm not, but that, too, is one of the ways the ALS Monster leaves its mark.

I continue to fight the Monster each and every day. It will keep chipping away at me and will continue to rob me of who I am, but I'm not going to let it give me bitterness, anger, depression or any other negative thoughts. I'll continue to smile inside at the thought of a family I love. I'll also smile deep inside knowing that life, all in all, is still good, even though the Monster keeps trying to defeat me.

Drunk

1/22/18

A bit over two years ago as I was losing my voice, I went through what I call my "drunk phase." That's because my voice sounded like I was drunk, which I wasn't. Now that I'm losing my ability to walk, I've once again entered into a "drunk phase." That's because unless I'm using my walker, I staggering like a drunken man. Even when I use a stick, I look and feel like I'm drunk. I assure you, I'm not.

A couple of weeks ago I started physical therapy hopefully to strengthen my legs and ankles. My physical therapist recommended I do five to ten repetitions of eight to ten different exercises. It's important not to over exercise, because exercising breaks down muscles that might not be able to repair themselves. Thus, it's a fine line between under utilizing muscles and over taxing them.

This last Friday I decided to hit the exercises a bit harder since I wasn't feeling any muscle soreness from the previous daily workouts. Instead of five to ten repetitions, I did fifteen to twenty. My legs felt fine, so I sat down to do a little work on the computer, and then took a short nap. The short nap turned into an hour, and when I woke up, my left leg and ankle hurt badly, and my lower leg and ankle were very swollen. I quickly texted a doctor friend, asking if he thought the swelling could be because I'm experimenting with blood pressure medications and my blood pressure was a bit high. He replied, that no, that could not be it. It didn't dawn on me that the swelling might be due to over exercising.

Later that same day my left leg was swollen, as was my right leg and ankle. The next morning both legs and ankles were back to normal size but both legs, especially the left leg, hurt like hell. And, my walking was worse than it had been just a few days before.

Then, yesterday, I noted that in just one week, my walking ability had gone way downhill. I've spent the last three days minimizing walking, and have done none of the physical therapy exercises. My legs feel better, but I walk like a drunken man.

So, do I exercise or not? My goal is to extend my ability to walk as long as I can. If I can make the leg and ankle muscles a little stronger by doing the physical therapy, that's good. But will even light physical therapy do more harm than good? This is a constant debate in the MND/ALS world. If you read the older literature, it says exercising is bad. But an equal number of articles say exercising is good, if you don't overdo it. So, starting tomorrow, I'll slowly work back into a few exercises. Only time will tell the outcome of this decision.

Walking and exercising make me feel better mentally, so that's a win. I definitely hope to keep walking a little longer. Meanwhile, if you see me staggering down one of the trails, please know I'm not drunk, even though I look like I am.

Fairness

1/24/18

My older brother, Fred, often says with compassion and love, he doesn't think it's fair that I have ALS. As humans, we often say something isn't fair when we try to empathize with those that are less fortunate than we are. So, when Fred says it isn't fair, I know he is speaking from the bottom of his heart.

A few months back a woman, who had been my pen pal for around 20 years, said she thought fairness had nothing to do with one person getting a rare disease and another, not. If you take out human emotion, mathematically, she is right. But, do we want to only live with mathematical odds, or do we want to show compassion for those less fortunate than we are? I'll go with the latter. I'll always do my very best to feel some compassion and empathy for others.

When I look at the British MND Facebook site that I follow, I often wonder why life is so unfair to obviously good people. It breaks my heart when I see a young woman with three young children living with ALS/MND, or a young woman who has a toddler and also MND. When I read about these people, I feel that life has not treated them fairly.

But I do not feel as if life has treated me unfairly. I've had a wonderful marriage for close to 45 years, three grandsons, traveled, had lots of adventures, always had enough to eat, never had to worry about shelter and I've never experienced a war first hand. I feel lucky, especially when I think about the two young women that I mentioned above, or read the news and see the horrors that living in a war zone imposes on the less fortunate.

ALS will continue to be a downhill slide for me and things will continue to be more of a challenge. This will put a greater and greater burden on my wife. That's when I question what is fair to her. She will just say "that's life," and she's right, but that doesn't mean I don't raise the fairness question.

To me, there are levels of fairness. Remember the photo in the news about a year ago of the five-year-old Syrian boy sitting in the back of an ambulance after he had survived a bombing. That photo epitomizes the height of unfairness. In the unfairness department, I'm light years away from that poor boy.

Life may not be fair, but it's been good for me, and I feel lucky for that.

Dental Care

1/26/18

A dental student recently posted on the British Motor Neuron Disease Awareness Facebook Group looking for information about dental care for MND/ALS patients. That post gave me the kick in the rear that I needed to sit down and write a little bit about the challenges of dental care in ALS patients.

I can only talk about this subject from my perspective, but other ALS patients probably face many of the challenges that I do. Because I can't verbally communicate with my dentist, the easiest way for me to "talk" about things is to list a few of them, and listen to how the dentist deals with them. Here is my latest list:

1. *Heightened gag reflex.*
2. *Can't open my mouth very wide.*
3. *Can't move my tongue.*
4. *Hard time breathing if lying back in a dental chair.*
5. *Choke on my own saliva or other fluids.*
6. *Anxiety.*

First off, I'm extra lucky that Dr. Marley, my dentist, is willing to work with my unique situation. It was his assistant that first suggested keeping the chair upright and tilting it back just enough that my head hits the headrest. This posture helps me breath better and lessens the chance of choking. Keeping a patient upright is harder on the dentist and his assistant, but I appreciate it. These two also recognize that spitting is impossible, so they are diligent about keeping enough suction to minimize fluids from running down my throat. They also give me plenty of very short breaks to let me tilt my head forward before I swallow. This helps keep my airway free. They also recognize that my heightened gag reflex requires that they take precautions, including using a gag reflex suppressant spray.

Post ALS, I've had my teeth cleaned five or six times, which is fairly easy and doesn't cause any anxiety. However, I've also had one filling replaced, a root canal and a crown installed. To combat anxiety of those procedures, Dr. Marley has me take a small dosage of the sedative Diazepam about a half hour before the procedure, and then he uses nitrous oxide just before he starts his work. He also minimizes the size of the rubber dam he uses, and he makes sure he cuts a small breathing hole in the dam.

Since my gag reflex makes it virtually impossible to take x-rays, this last visit Dr. Marley did a full CT scan of my teeth. He says he likes x-rays better for looking at a problem with an individual tooth, but the CT scan works. He also does more individual probing than he would if he had an x-ray. And since I can only open my mouth about half as wide as I could pre-ALS, his challenge of probing and doing dental work has increased substantially.

On the home front dental care is also a challenge. Dr. Marley's hygienist suggested that I switch to Reach Flosser, which looks like a toothbrush handle with replaceable floss on the end of the handle. I think that method of flossing is not only easier, but might do a better flossing job. I'm still able to use a regular toothbrush, but since I can't spit I have to let the toothpaste just run out of my mouth, which means I need to do a good face wash after brushing. I've considered using a three-sided toothbrush, but with the heightened gag reflex, I already have enough problem brushing, and I think the larger size would make brushing the back of my mouth impossible.

One speech therapist has me using mouthwash because the reality of aspirating food into the lungs is a high possibility. She tells me, if I do aspirate food into my lungs, I want to minimize the germs that are attached to the food. This lessens the chance of pneumonia. She suggested that I hold mouthwash in my mouth for a minute or more three times a day.

Were anyone to ask me for advice about dental care, I'd suggest they look for a dentist that is as willing to work with their disability as Dr. Marley is with mine. He has been a Godsend, and I don't know how I'd do without him. He has warned me that he will likely have to refer me to a dentist that specializes in hard-to-service patients. This means I'll have to fly the 1,000 miles to Seattle for dental care, so I hope he can continue to be my dentist for a long time to come. I sure appreciate what he has done for me.

Dennis Day

1/28/18

Here is a weird coincidence. My father liked a singer and radio personality by the name of Dennis Day. My father liked Mr. Day enough that he gave me the middle name of Dennis. I found out yesterday that Dennis Day died of ALS.

Emotions

1/29/18

It's 99.9 percent sure that I have bulbar onset ALS, but it's still up for grabs if I have Progressive Bulbar Palsy ALS, or possibly Pseudobulbar Palsy. Some neurologists don't consider Pseudobulbar Palsy a type of ALS. However, when you look up the Pseudobulbar Palsy Support Webpage, they say that ALS causes 50% of Pseudobulbar Palsy cases. There appear to be so many similarities between Progressive Bulbar Palsy and Pseudobulbar Palsy that it's hard to tell them apart.

One of the prominent symptoms of Pseudobulbar Palsy is uncontrollable emotional outbursts—either crying or laughing. I don't have these outbursts, but I'm much more emotional than I used to be, and sad things will often make me cry. With Pseudobulbar Palsy, the crying spells are usually unprovoked, and that's not the case with me.

To complicate things even more, I have had corrective surgery for Acromegaly [Acro]. Many neurologists think that the surgery just mitigates Acromegaly, and once you have Acro, you're never totally over the side effects of the disease. Acro patients suffer all sorts of maladies post-surgery. I'm lucky that I don't have to take supplemental hormones or drugs to control hormones like many Acro patients do.

To back up, here's a simple explanation of what Acromegaly is.

Acromegaly is usually caused by the growth of a benign tumor on the pituitary gland. Since the pituitary gland is known as the Master Gland that controls all the other glands in our bodies, the tumor can cause many imbalances in hormones. Usually the hormone that has the greatest imbalance is growth hormone, which causes adults to keep growing. Usually that growth is in the jaw, feet and hands, but not always. Growth hormone is just one of several hormones that can be thrown out of whack when a person has Acro. Surgery corrected my excessive growth hormone, but my testosterone levels are slightly below normal for a male of my age, though not low enough to warrant supplementing. So, could the low testosterone level be the cause of my heightened sensitivity to sadness? I don't think so. I do think my emotional sensitivity is another neurological abnormality.

Two or possibly three years before noticing my voice was failing, I seemed to be more empathetic to those less fortunate than I am. I'll be reading the news, see something that strikes me as sad, and tear up. Or, if I see a posting on Facebook where an animal is being mistreated, I'll tear up. Now if I see an abused animal posting on Facebook, I must cruise on by the post or I'll break down crying. But, I do the same if I see something tender, like a photo or video of a doe licking a newborn fawn. Or, the other night I was watching a documentary on friends that were separated during WWII. When they hugged for the first time in over 70 years, it made me cry big time.

Many men would not admit to being more sensitive, and would think that doing so makes them less of a man. I'm not ashamed of showing emotions that are normally associated with women. But, hey, I also wear pink shirts.

As for uncontrolled laughing, I don't do that at all. Connie might differ, because she will often hear me laughing for no apparent reason. The laughing is because something funny pops into my head, and since I can't talk, I laugh. I'll start laughing at something one of my grandsons has recently done. Or, our silly dog will do something that makes me laugh, and Connie doesn't see it. Here is an example. Just today at lunch Bella was licking out a bowl I put on the floor for her. The bowl moved just slightly, and Bella jumped about a foot high, thinking that something was about to get her. I started laughing, but this time I had to type into my phone what was so funny, and then Connie laughed too. Since I can't verbally share my funny thoughts, I often just laugh to myself, which can seem like I'm laughing over nothing.

Either laughing or crying can mess with my ability to breathe. In my case the old saying "die laughing," just might come true. Because of a compromised diaphragm muscle, I must be careful to not watch something on YouTube that is too funny, or my breathing becomes difficult. The same is true of something that is overly sad. While watching the PBS series Victoria the other night, when Queen Victoria's beloved dog died, I started crying and I had to turn away to get my breathing back in order.

I'm also not ashamed that I have ALS, and possibly other neurological disorders. And, I'll never be ashamed that I'm sensitive to sad things in the world. Just this morning while looking at the Facebook MND Support page I saw that a man I never even met a third of the way around the world, lost his battle with ALS, and I teared up. I could never feel the pain that his wife was feeling, but I did feel sadness for her, and as I write this I'm a bit teary again. No, I'll never feel shame for showing the emotion of sadness.

Downward Spiral

2/1/18

This morning I took a half-mile walk and it was nearing my limit of what I can do. By the time I was done walking the totally flat path, I was dragging my right leg. As hard as I tried, my leg would not lift up much beyond a drag. If I was observing this from the outside as a scientific observer I'd be fascinated at how rapidly the downward spiral has been lately. But knowing I'm observing myself, well, that's a different story. Just a month ago I was still able to walk a mile and half loop trail with some hills thrown in. I'm afraid those days are over.

I've tried not to be in denial about the inevitable path of ALS. However, I just can't see myself in a wheelchair, and I'll fight it as long as I can. I'm not sure why the idea of a wheelchair frightens me so much. Maybe it's because it will make me more dependent on others. Or, is it the fact that I've always loved hiking and walking? Or, possibly, it's because it's the precursor to more of the inevitable? It's probably all the above, and more.

At the end of the month we head to Seattle for more medical stuff. Since Seattle means the train from the airport to downtown, then lots of walking, and lots of hills we've been wondering how we are going to do it without a rental car or taxi. Connie suggested this morning that maybe we should get a wheelchair and she'd push me. Ugh! That is not what I wanted to hear. I've ordered a sitting walker or what I'm calling my All Terrain Walker (ATW) and I hope that will do the trick. The ATW should be here soon, and I'll practice with it and see if that makes walking easier. With the walker I'll be able to sit and rest if I need to, and at the worst, Connie could push me in the walker. So, I think we have this trip covered, but the trip after this one will require a wheelchair.

I shouldn't complain. After all, I'm four years into this journey, and that puts me into the realm of defying the odds of not already being confined to a wheelchair. And, I'm lucky that I'm still alive. None of that means I like the fact that a wheelchair will soon be in my future.

As I was losing my ability to talk, I found the best defense to keep away the blues was humor. So, I'm going to fight this with humor, too. I'm nearly twice the weight of Connie, and thinking of her pushing me up the hills of Seattle was envisioning her like the "Little Engine That Could" from the famous children's book. I can hear Connie now as we leave the light rail station and head up the hill to Virginia Mason Hospital "I think I can, I think I can." Then as we near the top of Seneca Street and the entrance to the hospital I hear her saying "I know I can, I know I can." When she read this, she said she saw herself nearing the top of the hill and falling backwards as the chair did a flip over her. We both laughed at that. I've also envisioned us going down to Pike Street Market, to Le Panier, our favorite French bakery. It's all down hill from the hospitals, and I can see Connie letting go of the wheelchair saying, "meet you there." I might as well see the humor in the situation instead of getting depressed about it. As the saying goes, "It is what it is." I can't do much about it, so I'll do my best to laugh, instead of cry.

Splitting Firewood

2/9/18

This might sound crazy, but I've always liked splitting firewood. Just as crazy—the sound that the wood makes when it splits is music to my ears. To me that sound is almost as delightful as a good Puccini aria. Yes, to many, the fact I like opera is even crazier than the fact that I like splitting wood.

As my ALS has progressed I've reached a point that I can't talk, can barely swallow, and walking is getting mighty hard. But, I can still split wood, and that makes me happy. Yes, I must admit that I'm only about one fifth as fast as I was pre-ALS, but I'm still happy that I can contribute a little to heating our house. It's less expensive to heat with the heat pump we installed a few years ago, but we like the wood heat. And nothing dries out a house in our wet climate like burning a wood stove. I look at the wood stove fire as maintenance on the house.

This is likely the last year that I'll be able to split wood, because breathing and getting down the stairs to the area where we split and stack wood is more and more challenging. Plus, my balance causes me to miss where I want to hit the wood about 25% of the time. In the past I almost never missed. My ever weakening muscles and lack of good balance makes swinging a heavy splitting maul harder and harder.

Anyway, I'm darn happy that I've been able to get out in the fresh air and do a little of what I've always like doing. To top off my good day, I only fell once and didn't get hurt in the process. My fall did give my wife Connie and grandson Blake a bit of a scare, but to me, falling is just part of life living with ALS, so no big deal.

Kids

2/10/18

The other day I was just about to lie down, when my seven year old grandson Dane, or as we call him, Lucky, came in from outside to warm up. As I sat on the edge of the couch nearest the wood stove, he put his back to the fire and started talking to me. Since, I can not physically talk I typed my part of the conversation into my phone, and for the first time ever, I let him read what I was writing instead of letting the app talk for me. I was getting a real kick out of watching him sound out the words and then verbally respond to me in his cute little voice. Just for fun, I threw in a few bigger and bigger words, and somewhat to my surprise, he figured out all of them. Yeah, I'm bragging about my grandson. Of course, it didn't take long for us to get silly, and he asked me to type in the alphabet and play it back to him. Funny, when you don't put spaces between the letters, the app says it as a long word. And funnier yet, it sounds Russian. He then asked me to type the alphabet in backwards and when played back, it, too, sounds Russian. As he laughed again and again, I jokingly typed into my phone that from now on "abcdefghijklmnopqrstuvwxyz, zyxwvutsrqponmlkjihgfedcba" was going to be his new name. This made him laugh even more, and I took delight in watching him having fun being silly.

After a bit more silliness, he asked me with a serious look on his face why I was sitting on the couch and not outside helping with a large family project with everyone else. I typed into my phone "sometimes, the disease I have robs my energy and I have only enough energy to sit on the couch." I'm not sure he can comprehend the idea of not having any energy. After a few seconds, he said in a serious voice, "Lots of people get cancer. Some people get cancer from smoking and some from drinking too much." After another pause he added, "Some people, like you, get cancer for no reason at all." This surprised me; I wondered why he thought I have cancer? I typed that I didn't have cancer, and with a confused look asked, "You don't?" I shook my head, "No," and he then asked what I have. I typed that I have a disease that messes with motor neurons in my brain and the messed-up motor neurons make my muscles not work right. His grandma walked in as he finished reading, and as he ran off he said, "I don't know what motor neurons are." If the subject comes up again, I will do my best to answer his questions without getting too technical—not that I could anyway.

I've read Facebook posts say it's okay to lie to kids about how to deal with diseases. I can't disagree strongly enough. I don't think it's ever okay to lie to kids, and as far as protecting them, is it really? I'm not saying you should burden kids with more than they can understand, but you should never lie to kids, even if it's not easy to answer their questions.

Shortly after I turned seven, the same age as Lucky, my mother died after an extended stay in the hospital. I was devastated, and clearly remember asking my father a day or two before, how she was doing. He told me that she was getting better and would be home soon. I'll give my father the benefit of the doubt and assume that he was trying to "protect" me from the sad truth. But I also remember the feeling that adults had been lying to me. So, it's not okay to lie to kids when someone they love is sick.

Two years ago, almost to the day, my neurologist told me that I had a motor neuron disease that was likely ALS, potentially bulbar onset ALS, and that I should get my affairs in order. The life expectancy for some with bulbar onset can be less than six months. Nonetheless, I knew that if any of my three grandsons asked, I was going to tell them the truth. I'm never going to lie to any child, especially my grandsons.

In a lighter vein, my grandsons have kept me in good spirits these last couple of years. Every day I chuckle about something they have said or done. Here are a couple of examples about Lucky.

When Lucky was around four and I could still talk, I went into our family restroom and I noted that one of the boys had left the toilet seat up. So, I went to the kitchen where they were all sitting and eating lunch and I said, "Boys, a true gentleman thinks about the ladies in the house and always puts the toilet seat down when done." Without missing a beat Lucky chimed in and said, "A true gentleman always goes outside and pees off the deck." Just typing this I laughed again. Also when he was about four, it had been well below freezing for several days. As he walked in the back door to our house, he announced, "A guy could freeze his nuts off out there today." I was a bit shocked to hear that coming from a four-year-old, and couldn't help laughing. I could hear his older brothers saying that, and he, of course, had picked it up. At seven, Lucky still makes me laugh each time I see him and I laugh and smile at all the silly things his brothers said and did, as well.

I've always had a soft spot in my heart for kids; especially young kids. Over the years I've been blessed to be around a fair number of young children and they always make me smile. I would do anything to protect any child, and most especially my grandsons. But, I'll never lie to them, under the false pretense of protecting them.

Handicapped

2/12/18

I never thought I'd be handicapped, and, I'm not ready to accept it now. But now I must use more and more handicapped ramps, handrails, walking sticks and a walker.

Last Friday evening Connie and I met our son Zach and his wife Jenn to watch a selection of the movies from the Banff Mountain Film Festival. Connie and I sadly missed the last three years of this Banff World Tour when it came to Sitka because we were out of town. So, I was looking forward to seeing the movies of outdoor adventures that I always enjoy. Unfortunately, I'd been too active during the day and had not saved the energy needed to sit though the full showing, so, by intermission I was tired and figured I'd best go home while I still had enough energy left to make it out of the auditorium and to my truck. Being handicapped, yes, I just admitted it, I knew that getting out of the auditorium was going to be a challenge. And, I was crazy enough to face this challenge without asking Connie for help. We live about four blocks from the auditorium, so Connie would walk home, but I should have asked her to help me get to the truck.

I was sitting at the end of the row, so I only had to stand up and make it down four stairs to the exit. To my surprise, though the building is fairly new, there are no handrails along the wall. I waited until the foot traffic had subsided, leaned against the wall and used my walking stick to help steady myself taking one step at a time without falling. It's much harder for me to go down stairs than up. Once I got into the main walkway, I had to make it to the double doors and hallway that lead out of the theater area. That was easier said than done, because people were rushing by on both sides of me. When I walk with a stick, I take up about 50% more space than the width of my body. In the main foyer I was met with a wall of people that formed haphazard lines to the restrooms, and looked as formidable as a line of riot police linked arm and arm trying to keep a mob back. How the heck was I going to get through that line—especially since I can't talk to ask people to move? My trick was to put my stick in between two people and inch my way forward until I worked my way through the forty or so feet of wall-to-wall people. Eventually there were gaps I could weave though.

I decided to exit the building via a long set of stairs I assumed would have few people. But, another event was just letting out of the adjoining high school, and I found myself in the middle of a horde of grade school and middle school aged kids and their parents. I immediately understood what it must feel like for a turtle crossing a busy highway. Have you ever tried to work your way through gaps of running energetic kids waving large foam hands that had #1 printed on them while trying to avoid small patches of ice on the sidewalk? By the time I got to the truck I felt like I was part of a video game with the odds stacked against me.

Saturday dawned clear with warm sun beating down for one of the first times this year. So Connie and I decided to test my new rolling walker on the Seawalk. After walking its length to the end of breakwater, we sat in the sun for 15 or so minutes before walking the ¼ mile back to our truck. Besides being flat, the Seawalk is wide enough for people to walk side by side with plenty of room to pass others. I tend to walk to the far right, as is my custom. A cute young boy of about three was heading right towards me on a bike with training wheels, and unless he or I moved we would have a head on collision. His mother was blocking my path to my left, so I exited the walkway and onto the grass. I wasn't upset with the young boy for blocking my way, but I was disappointed that his mother said nothing. Had the grass not been frozen, moving onto it would have been a challenge.

Nearly 30 years ago a controversy brewed shortly after the Americans with Disabilities Act (ADA) become law. Part of that law required spending public funds to make public areas more accessible. Some Letters to the Editor opposed sidewalk curbs being cut and ramped at intersections with roadways. Others were crying about more Federal regulations. I was fairly neutral on the controversy, but I'm sure glad the US Congress enacted that legislation. Another controversial saying is, "We are all just TABs, Temporarily Abled Bodies." Most of us, at sometime in our lives, will face difficulties being as mobile as we would like, so why not have compassion for those less fortunate and handicapped?

I could qualify for handicapped-permit that would allow us to park in a handicap spot. However, even when I transition to a wheelchair, I'm not sure I'll apply for the permit or plates. There are others that need the spots worse than I do, and so what if I must roll in a chair a few feet further? That said, it greatly upsets me it's when I see people who don't need them parking in designated handicap spots. An elderly neighbor of ours has a handicapped wife, and they have handicapped plates on their car because she needs them. But, I've seen him park in handicap places several times when she is not with him. He regularly walks his dog two or more miles or rides his bike, so, clearly, he is abusing the plates. And last summer I watched a mother with three teenage girls pull into a handicap spot. They got out of the car, walked up a half a dozen stairs and then literally ran across the street; they were clearly abusing the spots meant for others. We all cheat from time to time. We cheat on our taxes, drive a few miles an hour over the speed limit, or do a rolling stop at a STOP sign. But none of those infractions seem as wrong as an able-bodied person parking in a designated handicap spot.

As I become more and more handicapped I see that I took good health for granted. We are all but a heartbeat from a life-changing event. Enjoy your good health and please have compassion for those that are less fortunate.

Back

2/16/18

I'm not a hopeless romantic; I've always been more of a practical romantic. I had hoped to finish splitting some firewood as my Valentine's Day gift to Connie so that she could finish stacking it, but most of the day I lay flat on my back hardly able to move. On February 13th I messed up my back when I bent over to pick up a chunk of wood to split, and had to be waited on hand and foot most of the day. That's not what I was hoping for.

Possibly more painful than my back, is giving up one more thing I like doing. I can split wood if it's already stacked on the splitting block, but can no longer lift with my knees. This means I have to lift heavy things the wrong way. I'll ask my grandson Blake to split the last dozen pieces so as not to repeat the injury and let my back recover. He will make short work of splitting the last of the wood and will do it with a smile on his face, so I don't have to feel bad about asking him. But, that doesn't mean I'm happy about it. Once again, the ALS Monster is winning. UGH!

I've spent much of my life lifting heavy lumber and other things, so I'm used to a sore back from time to time. I never liked it, but also knew that it was just part of the job. In fact, I'm guessing you'd have a hard time finding a carpenter in my age bracket that doesn't know about sore backs. It's weird, but I yearn for the aches, pains, and even a darn sore back from doing manual work. If I experienced that kind of pain, it would mean I still had strength and muscles that worked, and that ALS hadn't robbed them from me. I'd even take a crushed disc in my back if I could give up ALS.

My leg muscles are now so weak they will hardly support me, and I have no wish to repeat the sore back experience. My arms are now so weak, it is nearly impossible to rollover in bed, let alone get out of bed. It seems the ALS Monster is giving me a little insight into what's to come. I don't like it, not one little bit. But, I'm also not going to live life afraid of what's coming next. I might be unable to finish splitting wood, just the latest in things I can no longer do.

ALS sucks, but life is good.

(When Connie read this, she said she would have appreciated the split wood. It was about as romantic as the vacuum I gave her for her birthday years ago. You can clearly see why I scratch my head in wonder about why she has stuck with me for these last 46 years?)

Therapy Wife

2/17/18

Our taste in documentaries is fairly eclectic, and last night, as we do most nights, we watched an hour and a half long online video on dogs. Our little beagle Bella was sleeping on my feet, throughout the full documentary, and, because our computer desk is very narrow, Connie was literally rubbing shoulders with me. Towards the end of the video they spent several minutes talking about therapy dogs and how they are so effective in helping people in hospitals, nursing homes and even hospice. The act of petting a dog can lower blood pressure, remove anxiety, and make people feel much better. I reached over and pretended to pet Connie's hair, and she turned to me and did a mock face lick, which made me laugh. Yes, we were being silly, but silliness and humor are good therapy. Just like the dogs that help patients fighting illness, the therapy of humor and love from my wife is the kind of therapy that keeps me happy. And, having a warm little dog that brings me such joy, lying on my feet also made me smile.

Even though I struggled to make our just over half-mile morning walk today, I enjoyed watching my wife and our dog. I get a big kick watching Bella get excited at the things she smells as she weaves back and forth waging her tail. And I get an equal kick watching and listening to Connie talk to Bella. Funny—when Connie talks to Bella, it's as if she was talking to a four-year-old child. And Bella is four. Again, this brings me joy. Even though some days the walk feels as if it's killing me, I get such pleasure watching the two of them, I'm not about to stop walking anytime soon. I enjoy it so much, even if I have to crawl, I'll keep on doing our walks.

When I read of the struggles some have living with a disease like ALS, I wish I could convey to them the importance of having someone to love and be silly with. I also wish I could tell them how important it is to have a pet to love. Love, humor and a family that includes pets are much better medicine than any drug. I feel blessed and lucky to have a therapy wife and therapy dog in my life. The two of them keep me laughing and smiling every day. I take joy knowing the ALS Monster can't take them from me.

Birthday

2/19/18

As I sit at my computer listening to beautiful Puccini opera arias, I feel compelled to write about my least favorite day of the year: yesterday, my birthday. I don't hate my birthday because I'm getting older. I hate it because of mental wounds and scars deep within my brain I've carried my whole adult life. Try as I may, I cannot seem to heal those deep wounds.

As an abused child, all I wanted to do was blend into the woodwork and never draw attention to myself. Abusers use birthdays to focus their attention on the person they want to abuse. The same is true for holidays, like Christmas, and if you have siblings, as cruel as it sounds, it spreads out the attention. When you share the beatings, your beating isn't as bad. This sounds equally cruel, but when you have someone to share beatings with, you also have someone to commiserate with.

Since my oldest grandson Blake's birthday is close to mine, and, because we are going to be out of town on Blake's birthday, we celebrated his birthday yesterday, too. I hoped the family would concentrate on his birthday and bring no gift for me. My wish did not come true. My son and his family mean well and the gift they made me was made with love. It was a simple gift—a birthday card signed by all of them with a collage of photos of themselves on the front of the card. This sounds unappreciative, but I could hardly look at the card and I passed it on as quickly as I could. I appreciate the thought and the photos. But the card made my birthday "front and center," and I could not blend into the woodwork. Blending in has been my mental defense for years, and I hate being the center of attention without doing something to earn that attention. The card is now hanging on the refrigerator, and I'll enjoy seeing the photos for the weeks that it's there. I'll do my best to disassociate the card with the day I hate so much, and enjoy the photos of the people I love. I also hope that if I live another year, I will not have to endure another gift. I HATE GIFTS that are given to me. Please, please, please – never again. It's just too painful. Please let me give gifts, which I like to do.

The brain is a complex thing—a thing the brightest minds in the world have yet to figure out. It's taken fifty-plus years of healing and trying to forget what I call the "Hell Years," to even begin to grasp why I hate February 18th so much. And, to add insult to injury, I can no longer talk. Why does that matter? When I could talk, I could quickly deflect the conversation from my birthday to something else. Yesterday, I wanted to say, "let's see what Blake got." And, though we quickly did, just not quickly enough.

When I sleep I always dream, and sleep and dreams are two things I enjoy the most. I often dream I'm back in school. In the dream I see myself as an adult, though most everyone else appears as kids. Last night was an exception I did not enjoy. For the first time ever, I saw myself back in grade school as a young boy, about the age of my youngest grandson Lucky, who is seven. Like most dreams, this one made no sense, except that I was dirty, bruised and in pain. In the dream I was trying not to stick out; I was trying to hide. Just before I woke up, I was crouched in a corner with my hands over my head. Someone was about to strike me with a stick and I was trying to scream, but of course I can't. I woke up and lay there for the longest time trying to self-analyze myself. I dug deep into long lost memories and remembered the physical and mental abuse from the "Hell Years." When I tried to go deeper, I couldn't. I think on one of those birthdays, I experienced something so painful that I can no longer dig it out of my memory. But, whatever that experience was, it still affects me. I wish I could erase it, but after fifty years, I think it's too deeply engrained to release me from the torture it inflicts.

ALS often leaves me fatigued, but yesterday I was more tired than usual. I'd guess the fatigue came from battles going on in my head, which left me depressed. And to make my not so very good day worse, my daughter-in-law's well-meaning mother, Carol, sent me a happy birthday email. I couldn't force myself to open the email upon receipt, and put off dealing with it and thanking her. I would have much rather been eviscerated and had rock salt poured on my innards than to respond to her email then and there. I am happy to report I opened the email and thanked Carol for her thoughtfulness first thing this morning. I'm also happy to report it was easy for me to do so the day after my birthday, and I suffered no harm.

For four or five years a few other volunteer divers and I trained with local city police and a few diving troopers for underwater body recover or search missions with the Alaska State Troopers Search and Recovery Dive Team. AJ, one of the diving troopers, had spent much of his career transporting prisoners from remote areas of Alaska to cities to face charges or transporting convicted prisoners to prison. He had been exposed to some very bad guys, and some with very serious mental issues. I once asked him how he dealt with the unruly prisoners, especially those with mental health issues. He said one technique was to act even crazier than they were. But the most effective way to control crazy wild misbehaving prisoners was to threaten to take away their birthdays. He said an over-agitated prisoner would often calm right down with that threat, and would behave for hours. If their behavior re-escalated, he'd just threaten again, with the same result. Oh, if it was only possible to take away my birthday. I'd sleep better if that were possible.

Postscript: In the years I was on the Search and Recovery Dive Team, I never got called to look for a body. My only mission was to search for a pistol thrown off a dock in downtown Ketchikan. The pistol had been used in an assault, and as the police went to arrest the guy, he tossed the gun off the dock in 60 to 80 feet of water. A city cop, another very good diver and I dove twice looking for the pistol, once during the day and the other at night. Night diving is actually the best time to look for something in the water, because your dive light forces you to concentrate your vision in one spot. We soon found that looking for the pistol was like looking for the proverbial needle in the haystack. The sea bottom under the docks in Ketchikan is littered with over 100 years of everything imaginable that could be tossed in the sea. There are old bits and pieces of boats, tons of used batteries, old marine toilets and hundreds of bottles and old aluminum beverage cans. The bottom also tends to be very muddy, and heavy things, like pistols, sink in mud. Neither we, nor any of the subsequent dive teams, found the pistol.

Getting Close

2/21/18

Getting close is often associated with good things. After a long trip it's always comforting when we are getting close to home. When we are hungry, we are happy when it's getting close to dinnertime. If we are tired, we are happy it's getting close to bedtime. And, as we approach the end of or careers we are excited to be close to retirement.

I'm now finding that there is a bad side of getting close. I'm now getting close to needing a wheelchair. Yesterday when we walked in the park, I was shocked at how much my ability to walk had deteriorated in just a week. ALS has robbed me of muscle strength slower than it does for many, so I feel lucky about that. But, I was still shocked until I thought about it. Four years ago, when my legs were in top shape, losing 1% strength wouldn't have been noticeable. However, today losing 1% strength when my legs are only a small fraction as strong as they were four years ago is very noticeable. UGH! I hate admitting that the wheelchair is just around the corner. But, I must face reality and as the saying goes, it is what it is. I can't do much about it, so I'll deal with it as best as I can and with as much grace as I can. As I've said before I'm not going to let the ALS Monster give me depression as it robs me physically.

Also bugging me is that I'm getting close to needing more and more assistance. I've never liked asking for help, and it bugs me greatly that the primary help is going to come from the woman I love. When you love people, it's hard to toss a burden onto their shoulders, and that's exactly what I'm doing to Connie. Five years ago we were excited she was getting close to retiring, which meant a new freedom for her, and me, as well. Now, as she is entering the years when life is supposed to be easier, my ALS will force a burden on her, one I don't want to give her. But she will just say "it is what it is." Or, "we will deal with it."

Since I can't talk, I've depended on Connie to make many contacts and enquiries these last couple of years. Today, she researched what Medicare requires to furnish a wheelchair, for when the time comes we are both ready for the physical part of the equation. I'm not sure either of us is ready for the mental part of that equation. I'm not.

As I've tried to do, though this ALS journey, I'll do my best to see some humor. It's at last become clear that Connie will get even with me for all the years that I out-hiked her. I can still see her on one of our first hikes in high school. Within an hour of hiking, she was two ridges behind me. For all these years that's been a joke between us. Now it's payback time for her, and I'm looking forward to laughing as I try to catch her in my wheelchair. I'm laughing right now, just thinking about the smile on her face as she tops a second ridge ahead of me. She claims she won't be smiling, but I disagree. I remember a hiking trip in deep, crusted snow. Because she is nearly 100 pounds lighter than I am, she could walk on the top of the crust while I was waist deep. She sure was smiling that time two ridges ahead of me. That thought makes me happy and I'm smiling knowing she is still healthy enough to out-hike most people half her age.

Walker

2/22/18

While I still can walk, I'll be using an outside walker that includes a seat. I was somewhat excited when the walker we ordered arrived, and I had a chance to take it out for a spin. My excitement quickly turned to disappointment because the walker was so poorly designed. Originally, we had asked for a less expensive walker, but the local dealer told us they recommended the one we purchased. She said that we should go online and see the ratings of the two different brands, and she was right – the one we ordered did have higher ratings. It was also about $80.00 more in price. According to the ratings, the one we bought had one-inch larger diameter heavier duty wheels than the less expensive one. Larger wheels make it easier to roll on rough surfaces. Also, the frame was heavier.

After trying it out within seconds I wondered what kind of idiot would design an outside walker with so many deficiencies? The brakes were either off or on. Imagine how difficult and dangerous it would be to ride a bicycle down a hill with brakes either off or on. I could modify them to work properly, making them apply a little drag. Then the harder you squeezed, the more drag would be applied and the brakes would work. In my basement shop we bent the steel part of the brake to hit the tire at an angle instead or straight. Bingo, the modification worked, and it was an easy fix. Why hadn't the manufacturer built it correctly in the first place?

Additionally, there was no way to lock the brakes, i.e., no parking brake. This is a siting walker. How was a person going to sit in the walker without it rolling? Connie sewed a simple Velcro strap, and the walker now has parking brakes. The walker will now be safer on hills and on public transportation.

One reason we chose a sitting walker is that if I get tired, Connie could push me. But there was nothing to rest my feet on—my feet would drag as she pushed me. Connie solved that problem by making a two-inch wide webbing belt that can be buckled just above the wheels. When I sit in the walker the belt puts my feet a couple of inches off the ground.

Sitting on it required another modification. When I adjusted the handles to the maximum height, the back of the chair was at shoulder height—not comfortable. This was easily remedied by drilling new holes in the frame to mount the seat back at lumbar height. Problem solved, but how could someone without the resources and tools that I have make these modifications? Didn't the design engineer check to see how the walker works in real life situations? Did they build a prototype during the design phase? Or did they go straight into production without seeing if the design would function properly? I used to build prototypes of new products, so I understand the importance of doing that in all new product designs. It seems to me that the manufacturer of this product forgot that important step.

After the improvements that Connie and I made to the walker, it is functioning like it should. I feel ready for our upcoming trip to Seattle where I'll depend on the walker to get to my many medical appointments. The walker is now working so well, in short spurts I can nearly walk as fast as a normal person. Yippee! Our modifications to the walker have transformed me into a "mean lean walking machine." I even added a bike bell to the handle bars. Watch out Seattle, you've been warned!

Staying Positive

2/23/18

Recently several people have commended me for having a good attitude, and some have asked how I stay positive when I have a disease that is slowly killing me. I'll answer the question with a question. What good is it if I'm downbeat, depressed, bitter, angry, or anything else that's negative? There is nothing to be gained by being anything that's negative, as negativity only breeds more negativity.

All too often I've watched bitterness and anger tear apart long-held strong relationships. What would be gained if I was bitter, and that tore apart my relationship with my wife? There would be no gain; wouldn't the destruction of years of happiness be biting the hand that feeds it [me]? My care in the future will depend on my wife, so why would I be foolish enough to jeopardize our relationship? And, why would I want to? I love my wife and don't want to bring any more misery onto her than the ALS Monster will bring anyway. I feel it's my obligation to do everything I can to help mitigated the negative, both for her and me.

It's not always easy to stay upbeat. Just today I felt myself slipping a bit into despair as my wife Connie was being proactive and asking financial questions about long term care. Potentially leaving my home to go into long-term care scares the crap out of me, and it would be easy to get depressed about it. It would also be easy to get mad at Connie for bringing up these subjects with our accountant, but I'm glad she is trying to plan ahead and look at all the options. Even something as depressing as the thought of ending up in an institution for long-term care is something that I just can't let get me down. I don't want to let the ALS Monster bankrupt us, so I do take comfort in knowing that Connie is looking ahead. Instead of dwelling on the negative of the reality that long-term care is a strong possibility, I'm happy that we are doing our best to ensure that Connie will be taken care of after ALS wins the battle.

I've watched disease and illness tear apart families, and I sure as hell don't want that to happen to mine. So, I keep looking at all the bright things in life, and do not dwell on my misfortune. If I start getting down, I dig into my memory banks and think about all the good times Connie and I have had together, or laugh at memories of all the funny things my grandsons have said over the last few years. Or I think about our silly little beagle, Bella. There are just too many things to be happy about to let the ALS Monster win.

Written Word

2/24/18

Other than body language and hand signals, the only way I've been able to communicate for over two years is with the written word typed on my iPad or phone app. My brain now functions much differently than before; it seems that the synapses in the language part of my brain have been totally rewired.

I see words visually in my brain when I think of what I want to say. Though I've always been an atrocious speller, I now seem to have a spell checker in my brain. My brain autocorrects words like "your" and "you're" before I type them. Weirder still, I often actually see words spelled out in my head, whether or not I intend to write them. Here's an example: pre brain-autocorrect, "Your not going to believe this, but they're going to deliver the fright today." Oops. Post brain-autocorrect, "You're not going to believe this, but they're going to deliver freight today."

Occasionally in my dreams I talk in the voice I recall before I lost my ability to talk. Now, more and more in my dreams, I find myself "talking" using the app on my phone, and I hear the same computer-generated voice that my phone speaks when I'm awake. Or I dream that I hand out a paper with my communications on it. The other night I dreamt I was standing in a house that my company was building. A half dozen carpenters and laborers were waiting for me to tell them their daily instructions. Before my ALS, that would have been a normal start to my day, so from that standpoint the dream made sense. Here's where it went off the rails; I handed a paper to each of the workers that said:

MEMO

It has recently come to my attention that there are too many high-headed nails out there. At your earliest convenience they need to be punched down. For those of you that don't know, the head is opposite the pointy end of the nail. Now, go grab a hammer and punch, and knock those buggers down 1/16" below the surface of the wood.

You can see why I woke up laughing.

In another dream I was driving a big rig truck with Connie in the passenger seat and our dog Bella sitting on the center console between us. On the dashboard of the truck there was a keyboard where the instrument panel should have been. I had to reach through and over the steering wheel to type my half of the conversation with Connie. She'd ask a question and I'd type a reply that was printed on an ink jet printer on the dash in front of her. She'd rip off the paper, read it, and then ask another question.

My English teachers would find it amusing that the written word has become such a major part of my daily life. I now know why they tried to pound the importance of proper sentence structure, punctuation and spelling into my head. Maybe I should offer my services to the local high school English teachers as a living example of why the written word is so important? Nah, like me at that age, the kids likely think they are invincible, and I don't want to shatter their illusion.

Accessibility

2/26/18

Until it became an issue for me, I never use to think much about accessibility. I always felt compassion for those less fortunate than I was, and, if I noticed, I'd offer a hand if I could. Now that I'm the less fortunate one, I'm seeing the things that I didn't see in the past.

Tonight, we met a friend for dinner at the restaurant in the hotel where we are staying. When the maître d' sat us near the back of the restaurant, I wondered how I was going to get out if the restaurant filled up? As we sat there eating and each table filled up, I saw the obstacle I'd have to confront to get out. If we didn't wait until the restaurant cleared out, we would have to disrupt a half dozen people to exit. Our friend, and then Connie stood up and started leaving. I wasn't panicking, but I was getting concerned. I clapped one hand on my leg and fortunately Connie heard me and came back. By collapsing the walker and having Connie hold my belt loop I'm happy to say I exited without falling over.

I'm guessing all handicapped people who depend on walkers or wheelchairs can relate to this story. Since I've had to depend on a walker I've experienced several similar experiences. Not talking exacerbates my problems. Tonight, if I could have talked, I would have asked the maître d' to sit us where I could get out if needed.

Yesterday we waited to exit the plane we flew to Seattle on until only a young couple with a baby remained. A very nice Alaska Airlines ramp agent met me at the door of the plane with my gate-checked walker. By the time I was slowly walking up the ramp, the flight attendants were debarking. In a wide spot in the ramp I migrated to the extreme right so two flight attendants could pass me. One of them jokingly said I only pulled over so that I could chase the pretty girls. I sort of laughed and as she passed. She then saw the bike bell on my walker and she said, "You know on the beach when the guys see a pretty girl, they ring a bell." As they sped away, I reached down and rang my bike bell. She then laughed and said, "You just made my day." If I could have talked, I would have said, "Yes, I can easily see my wife up there ahead of me."

I don't like becoming more and more handicapped. But, that little humor on the jet way has kept me chuckling off and on all day today. I don't remember who said, "always look on the bright side of life." Whoever it was has my admiration.

Dilemma

2/27/18

Warning: if you're squeamish about, or don't want to read about normal body functions, please skip this post.

I faced an interesting dilemma last night when I woke up at 3:00 a.m. Neither my wife, Connie, nor I was sleeping well in our hotel room. A massive muscle spasm woke me, and as hard as I tried, I could not get back to sleep. I swung my almost nonfunctioning legs over the side of the bed and after a struggle, using my legs as counter balances, I managed to sit up. After another few minutes of sitting and massaging the back of my leg that now feels more like an uncooked bag of spaghetti, I managed to slide off the bed and onto a chair. Here is where the dilemma started. I had to pee, and I didn't think I could walk to the bathroom with my walking stick. No big deal— there was an empty disposal drinking cup, and I could use it. But, then I began to feel other needs, and since constipation is now so prevalent, I figured I best head for the head. What to do? I thought about sliding off the chair and onto the floor, where I could then crawl to the restroom. But could I lift myself off the floor and onto the toilet? Both of my feet had been hurting like crazy, and just the thought of crawling made my feet scream in agony. I needed Connie's help, but I didn't want to wake her, since she'd been sleeping so poorly the last few nights. Ugh!

I heard Connie rollover and I could tell she was awake. I typed my problem into the speaking app on my phone and she got my walker. My walker would not fit through the door originally installed in 1928, so my dilemma was reborn. Now what? By partially folding up the walker, making it very unstable, I was able to make it to the toilet. Success. Well, not in the constipation department.

I'm laughing to myself about this crazy dilemma. It's either laugh or cry, and I think laughter is the better choice.

Jumping off a Cliff

3/2/18

Up until recently my decline from ALS has been slow compared to most ALS victims. I liken it to going down a set of stairs with lots of landings where my decline would taper off. A few times I'd jump down two or more steps to another landing where things would again become slow and steady. This week the stairs I've been going down ended on top of a cliff, and I've just jumped off.

Sunday I was using a walker that I hoped to use for many more months. That's not going to happen. Today I can no longer turn over in bed, can't stand unassisted, and walking a dozen feet to the bathroom and a dozen feet back, takes me 15 to 20 minutes.

It's been a very frustrating week. I've had to work overtime to keep positive, but I have. The biggest frustration came this morning. I hadn't eaten in over two days, so I was hungry. The nurses had not been told I could start eating again at 8:00. If it's not on their charts, they can't assume I was telling them the truth. They wanted to wait until the hospital floor doctor came around at 10:00. But when I was insistent and shook my fist to show I was getting angry, they relented and paged the doctor who had installed my feeding tube Thursday morning. A few minutes later I was able to order food, which arrived at 10:00, as did the floor doctor. Everything worked out. But when a person is as hungry as I was, the extra two-hour wait took me down a negative path.

Now I can laugh about it. The same doctors who tell me not to lose weight were starving me. I lost over five pounds from my normal weight. But because of water retention, I had gained about ten pounds. Thursday night they gave me Lasix, a very strong diuretic, intravenously, that had me up pissing away about two gallons of water. The same night they told me I needed to sleep. This irony has me laughing still. For four hours I was pissing into a portable urinal every five minutes. Surely some in the medical field have sadistic tendencies. If they say you need a good night's rest, they tell the night nurse to pump your veins full of Lasix. Sleep well, yeah, right. Ya' just gotta laugh at that.

Forced Education

3/3/18

Almost from the time we got up this morning, which was just before 5:00 a.m., we've been learning lessons on what it's like to travel handicapped. This education is being forced on us; it's not one we'd volunteer for. It is, however, giving me greater understanding and empathy for my fellow humans confined to wheelchairs.

Though the hotel where we were staying at is literally attached to the hospital, it has no handicapped-accessible rooms. If my walker wasn't going to fit into the bathroom, my wheelchair sure wasn't. Since I wanted a shower, I half collapsed the walker to get into the bathroom. Three days ago, I had been able to step into the bathtub with much difficulty. Could I do it again today? "ALS school" kicked in again. What I had done just three days before was now several times harder. And, harder means it takes more time. My half-hour shower wasn't enjoying standing under the spraying water; it just took longer to shower. What was a simple easy routine task a short ago is now becoming a mountain to climb.

Soon it was onto "Catheter 101 class," a class neither Connie nor I would have ever guessed we'd be taking. This special self-taught class had easy to follow instructions and a grade of pass/fail. If you feel piss running down your leg, you fail, if not, you pass. In our case we both deserve extra credit and should get an A+ because I gave it the ultimate test. In the airport food court I had to pee, so I did. No leakage. Yippee! It's strangely satisfying to piss in public; something I would have never known without ALS.

Why the catheter class? Most men in my age bracket pee a lot, maybe not in volume, but in frequency. I would not be able to sit in a plane for over four hours without taking a piss. And I couldn't get up to walk to the toilet. Please don't be shocked that I'd even bring up something as personal as a catheter. A lesson I keep learning over and over is, when you have ALS, modesty must be tossed out the window. This lesson came home front and center yesterday when a young female Patient Care Technician (PCT) in her mid-twenties helped my naked body into and out of the shower, dried me off and helped me into a gown. She offered to help with my underwear, but I declined. Even I'm not ready for that yet, and left that task for Connie.

The lesson continued. We are new to Uber, but I've always heard that it's reliable when it comes to the GPS selecting the pickup location. That's not correct and, I lost $5.00 for not canceling a pickup. The GPS showed on the screen correctly, but the Uber went to the wrong hospital entrance location, twice. Fortunately, the second driver called, and Connie got him to the proper location.

At the airport neither the driver, Connie nor I thought we should disembark at a curb cut. A nice Seattle policewoman helped us up over the curb, while mildly cussed out the driver for dropping us in the wrong location. Once through the airport doors a K-9 unit policewoman with a yellow lab quickly sniffed me on all sides, his tail wagging almost out of control. I could tell the dog loves his job. It wasn't until he pulled away that the policewoman smiled at me. I assumed the dog was trained to sniff out explosives?

Even TSA was a lesson. This was my first security check in a wheelchair, and I wasn't sure what to expect. Security seems even higher for a person confined to a wheelchair; just the seat cushion could hold enough explosives to do major damage. After thoroughly wiping the chair and me down with explosives sniff strips, he sent us in our way.

Then we learned more lessons about how clueless some are about the handicapped, and how little patience they have if a wheelchair is going to slow down their journey by even a few seconds. Some people are just plain rude. Today a woman and her young son of about five were standing at the bottom of a ramp blocking our path. After a few seconds she moved and then had her son move further into our path. Connie squeezed by him, without a word from the mother. She was totally clueless.

At the concourse we still had some time to kill, so Connie parked me in a very out of the way location while she went to the restroom and to look in one of the shops. Shortly after a young couple with a toddler came over and sat on the carpet in front of me. Soon the couple got into a big fight when the toddler fell and started crying. They carried on as if I wasn't even there. Was I really that invisible sitting there in a wheelchair? I've read where people who are confined to wheelchairs say they often feel invisible. This might have been my first experience with wheelchair invisibility.

Lastly, how do people get a person in a wheelchair onto a jet when there is no jet way? An adventure. An Alaska Airlines employee pushed my wheelchair, with Connie at my side, onto an elevator to the restricted aircraft ramp. Then a couple of hundred yards through a temporary construction barricade, open in the front, plywood roof and a plywood back, and a further distance across the ramp under the tail of the plane and to a meals service truck. My wheelchair could go no further. With two men helping me, I stood up and lifted my left leg onto the lift gate. Since I can no longer lift my right leg, I held on to the railing, one man held me, and the other lifted my now useless right leg up onto the gate. After Connie and two other people climbed on the gate, we were lifted to the bed height of the truck, where with the aid of one man, I walked just a couple of feet. Then the whole bed of the truck raised us to the jet's floor elevation. After that, the employee lowered the drawbridge and the two other passengers walked out onto the rear of the plane. I was strapped to an airplane aisle wheelchair, and wheeled nearly the full length of the plane to my aisle seat. The armrests were lowered, and I slid into my seat. The whole process took close to a half hour.

In case you are wondering, I used the catheter on the plane twice. If you urinate on ascent, the urine won't drain into the bag strapped between the ankle and knee. Smart guys only pee when the plane is level, or better yet, on descent.

This was a forced education. But the other catheter jokes kept Connie and me laughing all the way home. Just like the little piggies, I did go wee, wee, all the way home.

Toothpicks

3/6/18

When I look down in the shower I'm shocked at how skinny my legs have become. If my right lower leg weren't still fairly swollen, both legs would look like toothpicks.

About 20 years ago when Connie and I owned a climbing and fitness gym, occasionally I'd wear shorts. Frequently both bodybuilding fanatics and powerlifting guys would say something about how muscular my legs looked. They'd often ask what kind of workout I did to get such good muscle tone, and seemed shocked when I'd say: "walk."

John, one of the extra nice bodybuilding guys, usually came in midday, depending on how many carpet-cleaning jobs he had scheduled. Although we were on opposite ends of the spectrum politically, we became good friends. Most days after his daily workout we'd enjoy a cup of coffee and talk over local, US and world events. We seldom agreed but always respected each other's views. In the couple years we owned the gym we never got angry at each other. I especially liked that.

One day John didn't show up at the gym until late in the evening; something he never did. I was soon glad he came late that day. Connie had finished her workday at the Post Office, so when John asked me to join him in his daily workout I was glad I could say yes. Connie could cover the front counter for me and I could see how badly John was going to beat me up in the weight room. After a quick cardio workout, John and I hit the weights. Just looking at John's build there was no question who could lift the most or do the most repetitions. My back hurt just looking at the weights John stacked on his bar and the size of the dumbbells he'd lift. He was smearing me until it came to the leg workout. We were both surprised that I could not only keep up but could out lift him by a major amount. On both the leg press and the leg curl machines, it was as if John was in the minor league and I was in the majors. I seldom used the weight room, whereas he used it five or six days a week. He couldn't believe me when I said my legs got strong just from walking and climbing on the climbing walls. My leg muscle tone he so admired was gained because I walked, loved to hike up hills and loved to climb. When I told John all he would have to do if he wanted the leg tone I had was to walk, you would have thought I asked him to cut off his arm. Funny—he had the self-discipline to workout daily, but not the self-discipline to walk. I even invited him to join Connie and me on a scenic walk around Ward Lake, where we could enjoy the smells of the forest and watch for wildlife. In all our political conversations John and I had no hard feelings. But asking him to enjoy a walk outside was like a slap in the face.

Now that ALS has turned my legs into toothpicks, I wish with all my might that I could enjoy a nice walk through the forest. But, I beat the odds. I walked longer than I might, or possibly should have. A good doctor friend said he thinks my determination and persistence is what extended my walking as long as it did. I think he is right. Now I'm going to do all I can to hold off getting an electric chair. I want that determination and persistence to keep my arms working as long as possible.

Letter to the Doctor

3/7/18

Because I can no longer talk, I almost always write a letter that we hand to a nurse to give to whatever doctor I'm seeing. Two weeks ago our local primary care physician and internist, Dr. Hunter, asked me to check with him because he has been adjusting my blood pressure medication. Plus, he knew we were traveling to Seattle, and he always likes an update after each visit. This way he knows what medical records to request from the Seattle Hospital.

I am lucky that we have such a good caring primary care doctor. Dr. Hunter is one of the reasons we can continue to live here, where we want to live. This is a little longer than the typical letter, because so much has changed in two short weeks.

To: Dr. Hunter

Regarding: Marcel LaPerriere

As you can see I'm now in a wheelchair. This is because of muscle loss in both legs. The right is the worst. I can move my right leg only very slightly, and to lift it when sitting I must use my arms to assist in the lift. The walker is now limited to very short distances from the bed to the toilet, which is less than 15 feet.

A few days before we flew to Seattle on the 25th of February, my legs started swelling badly. By the end of the flight my legs, especially the left was, extremely swollen from the knees down. By the 27th when I saw pulmonologist Dr. Horan, the main swelling had shifted to my right leg and my big toe was nearly twice its normal size. Dr. Horan was concerned about blood clots and after a blood test showed my D Dimmer level was high at .72 she ordered an ultrasound on both legs. The ultrasound came back negative.

On the 28th we attended an ALS clinic where the Respiratory Therapist, along with another Pulmonologist, Dr. Steve Kirtland, determined I was past due on using a BIPAP machine [a ventilator that helps breathing]. I need to start using one at night and, in time, will likely need it full time.

During the ALS clinic we first saw Dr. Kirsten Gage, Rehabilitation Medicine, and she put me on Mirabegron 25mg. That will hopefully reduce the number of times I need to get up in the night. Also, Omeprazole 10mg to prevent heartburn and it's working great.

The last person we saw during the ALS clinic was the new ALS doctor, Neurologist, Dr. Xuan Wu. She poked, prodded, and checked my range of motion and reflexes. By this time both my feet had swollen massively and the pain on a scale of 1–10 was spiking in the 8 to 10 range. Two things I found interesting.

1. *I forget what she called it, but when she checked reflexes the opposite leg also responded.*

2. *The same when she would stimulate by rubbing one leg the other would start convulsing right above the knee and would start wiggling like the leg was full of Jell-O.*

By the time we were finished with Dr. Wu, who I very much liked, we'd been in the same examination room for over 4 ½ hours. Walking with the walker as we left was unbearably painful and I only made it maybe 250 feet before Connie had to push me in the sitting walker. By the time we got back to our hotel room, less than 10 minutes later, I was going into a mild shock. Uncontrollable, shaking, rapid breathing, flushed skin and sweating, even though I was cold. The ALS nurse sent for Transport and they took me to the ER. Everyone who saw me in the ER was very concerned about the swelling and pain. Plus, my BP was skyrocketing. Blood test, chest X-ray and CT scan, again showed no blood clots. I was given an IV dose of Lasix and from midnight to around six in the morning, I urinated over 4 liters. That helped bring the swelling down.

March 1st, they installed, as Connie calls it, the through hull fitting, but the medical folks call it a PEG. All went well with the procedure. More blood tests and several doctor examinations later, they figured the swelling was caused by a failure in my skeletal muscles to the point my heart can no longer pump the blood back up my body. Liver, kidney and heart tests all showed normal. As the swelling continues to go down the pain has subsided.

The hospital rounds doctor, Dr. Biebelhausen, put me on a nightly dose of Gabapentin 300mg for nerve pain. He also increased my Baclofen from 5mg to 10mg. The combination of the two drugs has help with night pains. I was discharged on the afternoon of the 2nd and we flew home on the 3rd.

I now wonder, if the left leg swelling I had a few weeks ago was caused by the same thing?

I hope you can help with me get these things I need.
- *A prescription for a hospital bed.*
- *Someone to professionally adjust the wheelchair was given to us by the ALS Association. They suggested professional adjustment.*
- *Food for the PEG. Connie will have questions.*
- *Solutions for PEG leakage and prevention of associated infection.*

Connie will fill you in on what we know about the BIPAP at this time.

New Drugs:

Gabapentin 300mg
Omeprazole 10mg
Mirabegron 25mg
Furosemide 20mg (if swelling gets too bad, take one per day.)

Caregiver

3/9/18

I would never wish ALS, or any disease, on my wife. But, I often wish our roles were reversed. I wish I were the caregiver and not she. ALS, or any disease, can be harder on the caregiver than the person receiving the care. In my case my poor wife has been loaded with not only all the caregiving, but tasks that used to be mine. Case in point, as I write this Connie is outside shoveling snow. Since Connie retired as few years ago I haven't helped much with cooking dinners, but I've mostly gotten my own breakfasts and lunches. Now, more and more of those tasks are also falling on her shoulders. I can't even help load the dishwasher from my wheelchair.

The other day while napping, I awoke to the sound of a chop-saw cutting wood in my basement workshop. I'm married to one of the most talented women on the face of the earth, but, just like I have zero sewing talent, Connie hasn't much aptitude in carpenter skills. Nonetheless, she was in the shop modifying a set of stairs so our little beagle, Bella, can get on and off the higher bed I'm now using. (She did a great job too.) Connie has had to take up more and more duties that would have been mine pre-ALS.

I feel guilty that my disease has shifted so many additional duties onto Connie's back. The time she spends taking care of me or doing the tasks that I used to do robs her of fun things she likes to do. It's not my fault that I have

ALS, but that doesn't mean I don't feel guilty. I love my wife too much not to feel guilt for what my disease is putting her though.

All too often I read where caregivers burn out, and I can see why. Besides all the extra work that is thrust on them, they are also burdened with extra stress. Last night at 3:00 a.m. some strange noise in our house woke Connie. She ran down the stairs to see if I was okay, which I was. Whatever the noise was, it interrupted Connie's sleep. Once we get a hospital bed for me, we will be sleeping in the same room again. I hope that helps relieve some of the worry Connie lives with 24/7.

I'm lucky I married such an amazing woman. Hopefully we can find the right balance—a life other than endless taking care of me and taking on more and more of my former duties. Fortunately our little town is blessed with many resources that will help both Connie and me as my ALS progresses. We haven't used any of those resources yet, but we will. I feel good knowing they are out there, when we need them.

In this country we honor all sorts of people for all sorts of things. Mother's Day, Father's Day, even Grandparent's Day. There is even a National Caregiver's Day. If you asked 100 people on the street what day of the year we honor Caregivers, maybe one would know. I've always known how special caregivers are, but being the one who now needs care, it's easy for me to see that caregivers are greatly under appreciated. I can never thank my wife enough for all she does for our home and me. If you know a caregiver, please thank them, and if you are a caregiver, here is a big thank you from me. Those of us living with ALS couldn't do it without the dedication that caregivers selflessly commit to us daily.

Stairs

3/10/18

When I came down the stairs from our bedroom to leave for Seattle on the 25th of February, little did I know I'd never again go up those stairs again. The ALS Monster keeps taking things from me. Some hit me harder than others, and not being able to manage stairs has hit me like a brick on the head. Rating the loss of capabilities on a scale of 1–10 with 10 being the worst, the loss of being able to go up and down stairs is right up there at an eight or nine. In comparison, losing my ability to drive is maybe a three or four.

In the autumn on 2007, we were finishing building our house after close to two years of long hard hours. In the mid '80s Connie and I had done what some say is the biggest test of a relationship; we built a 45-foot sailboat that we lived on for 21 years. As overwhelming as it was to build a boat, that project paled in comparison to building this house. The house project was truly a family project. Connie and I acted as the general contractors and we hired our son Zach as the sub-contractor to do much of the work. All during construction Connie had a very stressful full-time US Post Office job and I had a more than full time job, working 50 to 60 hours a week. With some hired help, Zach worked 50-hour weeks on the project, Connie averaged around 20, and I worked 20 to 40 hours a week on the house. Other than the excavation work and the screw pilings the house sits on, we did not subcontract out any of the work. From foundation, to framing, to roofing, to wiring, to plumbing, we did it all. That we built the house with our own blood, sweat and a few tears gives our home a special place in our hearts. And, now of three floors, I can only access the main floor. That's why I rated the hit on the loss scale as high as I did.

After Connie's father passed away in 2005, Connie's mother Millie came to live with us here in Sitka. That ended our boat life, and we started looking for a house to buy. Millie would be moving from a house where she enjoyed an amazing 360-degree view, bathed in the nearly endless Colorado sun, compared to our near constant rainy Southeast Alaska. We knew that we had to find a house that enjoyed sun when we get it, and it had to have a view. It had to be a house with big windows and lots of light. After looking for a couple of months we realized the only way we'd get what we wanted was to build. Also, the houses that were on the market were cheaply built, and I wasn't going to settle for that.

We got extra lucky with the lot we ultimately purchased. It had been for sale off and on for around 25 years, and because it was tricky and unusual, hadn't sold. It sat about 20 feet lower than the road and was covered in heavy brush and trees growing on what we call muskeg, technically a bog. The surface can be walked on, but it feels spongy. You can't build a house on that kind of soil. The normal course of action is to dig through the muskeg to bedrock, and then fill with quarried rock. This lot is lakefront and sat only few feet above the lake surface. We could not dig out the mushy soils without the lake running into the hole, and our neighbor's house might migrate towards our hole as well.

Luckily, a couple of years before we purchased the land, I had learned about helical piers—sometimes called screw pilings; the solution to building on this tricky lot. We would screw helical piers thorough the mush until they hit bedrock. This meant lots more foundation work and a fair bit more money. To get the house closer to street level for access that didn't require stairs, we had to elevate the lot by bringing in lots of rock. Foot access would be via an elevated deck. Again, more work and more money.

As we started construction, a couple different people stopped to tell us that they had wanted to buy the land but couldn't figure out how to build on it. One lady even said she and her husband consulted with an engineer who said the lot was impossible to build on. I'm glad that engineer didn't know what he was talking about.

As construction started, it became clear the house was going to be a major project. We knew that theoretically, but somehow pre-construction optimism is not the same as reality. And the weather—through much of the project we had record or near-record rain and snow fall. Yes, we had some very stressful days, but the project rewards were tenfold greater than its negatives. After all, it was a family project. Even Millie seemed to be excited about the project. When her kids were young, she and her husband, George, had purchased a piece of land with the intention of building. But before they built, a good deal on a house came along. They bought it and raised their children there. I think Millie still had a dream of building a home, and seeing the slow but study progress seemed to make her happy. She always enjoyed it when Connie would bring her by. We'd walk through the construction pointing out where things would be. Millie's excitement grew as we neared completion and she could see where her beloved dining table would sit and how her bedroom would be arranged. I think the frosting on her "cake" was getting to pick the color of her room, the draperies and even the vanity in her bathroom. The big day came in October of 2007 when she moved in—she was all smiles.

I'll back up to June of 2007. The small liberal arts college where I worked closed their doors and 110 of us got pink slips that day. But since my job as Maintenance Director was deemed essential, I was hired back within minutes of being laid off. That was good, since Connie and I were building an expensive house with mounting bills. Unfortunately, my boss, who I very much liked, wasn't rehired, and I began reporting directly to the President of the school. That President was a full-on narcissist, who, to my mind, was the cause of the school's demise. Since I no longer had my boss to insulate me from him, I knew I wouldn't last long, and I didn't. When I scheduled a meeting with our bank loan manager, she gave me what might seem like strange advice. She said that she knew we were good for the money. She thought I should quit and concentrate on finishing the house. After the house was completed, then I should worry about making money. I took her advice and by July, I was doing what I wanted to do, working on the house.

I was happier not working for a person who had literally killed the college, and I was working on the house. Seeing the daily progress was rewarding. By directing my energy towards the completion of our house gave me time for finishing the wiring, plumbing, and it also freed me for fun projects like building the stairs that would lead to the balcony, our bedroom and Connie's sewing room. These stairs are not some grand entranceway showpiece, but they are one of the focal points in our rustic Alaska great room.

That I built the stairs is not the only reason it hit me hard when I could no longer go up them. The stairs also represent many good memories. I remember when five-year-old Blake asked for a "spy" window to be framed into the loft above the sewing room so he could spy on adults in the great room. He also picked the color, and with Connie's help, painted the loft. After construction was completed, I sat many hours at my computer desk on the balcony listening to Connie and her mother Millie laugh while they worked crossword puzzles. Those stairs represent love and family. From my balcony perch I could also see that we had done well, because Millie always enjoyed sitting in her chair looking at the view out the window. It wasn't like the view she had lived with for so many years, but she enjoyed seeing ducks, swans, herons and bald eagles land on or near the lake daily.

I'm also upset I can't use the outside stairs to get to my basement workshop. I've always loved building things, and the ALS Monster has taken that from me, too. Also, if I can't go down the outside stairs, I can't access the lake or dock I built with one of my employees. I can still look out the window, but that's not the same as lying on the dock on a sunny day.

I'm taking the loss of the ability to navigate stairs hard. Since we built this house with the first floor being handicapped-accessible, a stair lift would seem like a waste of money. We built the main floor to be handicapped-accessible with my mother-in-law in mind, and which she used. Now I need it, even more than she did. I would never have thought it would be me who needed the ADA ramp to the garage, or the walk-in shower. But it is, and the added expense that we thought we were investing to make life easier for Millie turns out to benefit me.

I've said it before and I'll say it again. The ALS Monster tries to give me bitterness each time it takes something away from me. But I'm not going to let it. I'm still looking at all the positive things I have in my life, and they far outweigh the negative. I'm still a happy camper, all be it one in a wheelchair. I look back with satisfaction at our lovely home, knowing it was our hands that built it.

Shortly before my father-in-law George passed away, he asked me to take care of Millie when he was gone. I was honored he asked me though he didn't need to. Connie and her mother always shared a bond that I think is only possible between a mother and daughter. I love my wife and always looked at my in-laws as parents. Of course we would take care of Millie.

We undertook major life changes when Millie came to live with us in Sitka, and we are now benefiting from them. When we built our sailboat, Terra Nova, we figured we'd live the rest of our lives on that boat sailing around the world. Over time that dream was downsized to spending our lives exploring the waters of Southeast Alaska and British Columbia. When Millie came to live with us, we once again modified our plans and built this magnificent house. I'd hate to think of what life would be like now if we had not built this house. I'm not happy that I can't use the stairs, but I'm darn thankful for the house I live in with the most wonderful woman on earth. Despite the fact the ALS Monster has once again robbed something from me, I'm smiling because I've have things darn good.

Pronouns

3/11/18

They say the first step in a recovery is to admit you have a problem. Okay, I admit it. I listen to too many podcasts. There, it's out in the open. However, I'm not about to reform my habits. I like podcasts because they're a good way to keep up with current events. Plus, I like the adventure stories I hear, I like leaning about people I admire, but mostly, I often learn things I otherwise wouldn't.

The other day I learned that how you use pronouns can tell you about your personality or others'. When I thought about it, it made sense. A person who almost exclusively speaks or writes using the word "I" is apt to be a narcissist. Even more interesting, a person who fixates on "I," especially in poetry, is very likely to commit suicide. But someone who uses "I" frequently and throws in a fair amount of "we" or "us," is often a happy person. I frequently use "I' but, I'm happiest when I add in "we" or "she" when I'm talking about my wife, and "our," when talking about our grandchildren, other family members, or friends. Point proven.

Per that podcast, people who use "them" or "they" more than "I," "me," "us," or "we," tend to be paranoid. I use those pronouns infrequently, so I guess I'm not paranoid. I don't talk of myself in the third person either, which is also a sign of narcissism.

Since ALS has forced me to rely on the written word, I will be cognizant of my choice of pronouns. When I write in the first person about ALS, I'll continue to use "I," and to make sure the reader understands that I'm happy, I'll continue to add in "us," "we," "our," and of course, "she" and "her."

Who knew the use of pronouns could tell others about who we are? I didn't.

Balance

3/12/18

Today is what I call a "P Day." That's because at breakfast I downed a strong diuretic pill called Lasix. That pill not only starts many trips to the restroom, but it starts a balance game of trying to get rid of the excess fluid in my swollen legs and feet while staying hydrated. That's not an easy balance to achieve.

Quoting from Wikipedia: "The skeletal-muscle pump is a collection of skeletal muscles that aid the heart in the circulation of blood. It is especially important in increasing the venous return to the heart but may also play a role in arterial blood flow." Because of ALS my skeletal-muscle pump has been compromised. Fighting gravity to get blood and fluids up from my legs and feet is now more than my heart can do. Hence, the swollen legs and feet. And the swelling equals pain; more swelling, more pain. It becomes a balance. Do I sit in my chair or lie in bed to mitigate the swelling? I'd go crazy if I lay flat on my back all day, so pain vs. mobility is also part of the balancing equation that I'm playing today. My right leg is swollen so much I'm guessing that tomorrow and maybe the next day will also have to be P Days.

Today, sitting at my computer, I realize all the things that I took for granted just a couple of years ago. Eating, drinking, talking, walking and now even blood flow though my body. If I could turn time back, I'd live each day as fully as I could. I'd cherish being able to eat my favorite foods, or, being able to get enough liquids in a day without having to use a PEG feeding tube to inject water into my stomach; walking and standing upright, or being able to carry on a verbal conversation. But my heart is still strong, my kidneys work properly, and my lungs still provide me with enough air to sustain life. As much as ALS sucks, life is still good.

Beds

3/13/18

"Advocate" could also have been the title of this update, because only Connie's endless diligence as my advocate got me, at long last, a hospital bed. Connie most probably lost track of how many calls she made. For four years Connie has been my advocate for literally everything. Neither of us should be surprised at the hassle by this time. Literally every doctor, nurse, physical therapist, and on and on, said I need to get a bed that would help me sit up. In other words, a hospital style bed.

The bed arrived yesterday afternoon, and it's wonderful. Last night was the best nights sleep I've gotten in a couple of weeks. Connie also slept better, because she moved her old brass bed from her childhood next to my bed. She can now sleep better knowing that she is only a couple of feet away if I need something. And our little beagle, Bella, was happy that we were both in the same room again. The canine instinct of keeping the pack together is so strong in Bella; she didn't know what to do when we were sleeping in different rooms. Last night there were three happy people all enjoying a good night's sleep. Bella is a dog, but to us, she is our little girl, so that makes her human in our book and I think in hers too.

Just before dozing off, I thought of the various beds we've had during our nearly forty-six years together. For twenty-five years, or over half of our time together, we lived on three different sailboats, with twenty-one years on our last boat, Terra Nova. There is something special about sleeping on a boat, and except for a few stormy nights, we always slept well. One very windy night we were anchored in a not very protected bay, about as far from civilization as one can get. The winds were gusting at near one hundred miles per hour. Poor Terra Nova would heel over, her decks awash, then shake and shutter with each gust. We didn't sleep well that night, but we were glad to be warm and dry in our well anchored boat, and not out at sea.

In1975 on our first sailboat, Nimbus, a cheaply built fiberglass boat with leaky decks, we were often wet in our not at all comfortable bunk. We first moved aboard that boat when moored to a dock on the Seattle Ship Canal. Because of nearly endless boat wakes twenty-four hours a day, Nimbus never sat still. Sleeping was sometimes a challenge as the boat rolled one way then the other; she'd jerk to a stop as the mooring lines came tight. That sudden jerk is not conducive to good sleep. Zach, just a toddler then, loved his quarter berth under the cockpit seat. He called his bunk the "cave," and he'd spend hours crawling to the depths of that bunk with a flashlight playing with his stuffed toys, and toy trucks. The constant motion never seemed to bother him like it did us. He seemed disappointed when we moved to a protected dock behind a breakwater. Maybe it was the early boat life that gave Zach his sea legs that kept him from getting seasick when I'd be puking my guts out.

When Connie and I were first married, we lived in a furnished apartment in the South Park section of Seattle. By the time we paid rent and bought groceries, we had very little money left over. To save a few dollars on rent we asked the landlord to make it an unfurnished apartment, which he did. We'd found a used furniture store within easy walking distance of our apartment and they let us make easy payments on furniture, less than we paid to rent furniture in our apartment. To save even more, we got a couch with a fold down back that would double as our bed. The first night we made the couch into a bed, and lay down to sleep. Soon after, I scooted a little too close to Connie, and she got dumped onto the floor as the couch tipped over. During the six months we used that couch as a bed, we had to be extra careful or poor Connie would get dumped on the floor. I'm not sure what was more disruptive to our sleep—Connie being dumped or the two of us laughing about it.

As my ALS progresses, it becomes more and more of a challenge to not be depressed or bitter. All the good memories that Connie and I have together are what keep me upbeat and sane. I love lying in bed recalling the fun adventures we've had together, and it's those memories that will always be stronger than the ALS Monster.

Will the bureaucracy kill me?

3/15/18

Fifteen days ago, March 1, 2018, both a Respiratory Specialist and a Pulmonologist determined that I was way past due for a breathing aid called a Bilevel Positive Airway Pressure (BIPAP). Two days after, March 3, 2018, they prepared a prescription for the machine so that Medicare and my insurance would pay for it. That prescription was faxed to a company here in Alaska that would supply the machine and give training on how to use it via Facetime. Through various bureaucratic snafus, the order remains unfilled. "We didn't get the fax." "They sent it to the wrong number." "We got the fax, but it has the wrong code number on it." "The insurance numbers are wrong." And on and on. Poor Connie has been run ragged with phone calls to the company and Virginia Mason Hospital in Seattle. Everyone seems to be pointing the finger at the other guy and the process has stalled.

The number one killer of ALS patients is respiratory failure. A mild cold can lead to death. I have either a mild cold or a bronchial infection that seems to be worse at night. And night is when I really need the BIPAP. Two nights ago we nearly went to the ER, but my breathing improved using the nebulizer, and all was okay. The BIPAP sure would have been nice. There's just something about breathing that's kind of nice.

Needing to go to the emergency room is also a bit of a dilemma. Sitka, a town of 8,500 people, has a regional native health hospital and a community hospital. We've had bad experiences with both hospitals. The community hospital screwed up time sensitive blood tests and over-charged for an infusion by 100%. Then the native hospital misread a CT scan and totally missed the blood clots in my lungs. And the MRI they did was unreadable by Virginia Mason. Reliable sources say the ER is better at the community hospital, but the native health hospital has better equipment and a bigger medical staff. It's a crapshoot either way. I can see why people move south when they have a serious condition. I'd rather be dead than leave Alaska.

Having an advocate is crucial; without Connie, I'd be dead. As the saying goes, "The squeaky wheel gets greased." Connie keeps pointing to several squeaky wheels that need attention. Without success on the BIPAP soon, I won't be writing any more posts.

Experts

3/18/18

My son Zach posted a photo of a beautiful bowl he had just finished turning on Facebook. He had left the edges on the top of the bowl sharp, and said that expert wood turners say that the top edge of the bowl should always have a radius. I commented, "Not all experts are experts." That's true in the medical field too. So, what is an expert?

My first major lesson in experts was as an apprentice machinist in the early '70s working for a Seattle company that sold and repaired machine tools. We'd also build special machines and tooling for machines. A special tooling jig we built was a fixture to hold the rough castings that would be machined into fire hydrants. A Washington State licensed mechanical engineer who had been designing tooling for longer than I'd been alive designed the fixture. By all engineering standards, he should have been an expert in his field. The fixture he designed had a major flaw I saw early on, as I machined the parts to make it. I showed the flaw to my boss and he instructed me to finish the work, after which we'd address the problem. The completed fixture didn't work. I knew there was a simple cure, and with permission from my boss, made the modification. By golly, it worked great. When the expert saw my modification, he blew a gasket and made us remove it, making the tooling totally worthless. Rather than admit a "wet behind the ears" young tradesman could make his design work better, he designed a series of modifications that made his tooling somewhat work and awkward to use. After we delivered the tooling to the company that was paying for it, we heard that the machine operators machining the fire hydrants hated it and that it added time to the manufacturing process. It may have been one of the reasons that company moved their manufacturing to another firm—maybe Mexico. The failure was because an "expert" wasn't as much an expert he claimed to be.

I've worked with many engineers, some just like the guy mentioned above, but also some darn good ones, too. The best, the ones I'd call experts, are those who learn from their mistakes, are open to ideas, and have gotten their hands dirty doing work in their design field. Poor engineers have only "book learning," and won't listen to anyone. In Sitka we have one of the finest structural engineers I've ever seen. He has become really good at what he does by doing the things I listed above. He's a true expert in his field. He got that way through experience and his willingness to learn.

A nice young man who graduated from Sheldon Jackson College a couple of years before I went to work there stayed in Sitka and, like many young graduates do, went fishing. I first met him when the boat he was working on broke down in a bay about ten miles out of town. His wife, through my son, asked me to take our boat out to get him, because he was needed back in town. I did, and during that chat returning to Sitka, he told me his father was a big-time house building contractor somewhere on the east coast of the US, and he was thinking of going back to work for his dad. I said something to the effect that the move might be a good way for him to learn house-building trades. He and his wife did move back east, and he went to work for his father.

He returned to Sitka in about three years. Sheldon Jackson had closed and Connie and I had started our construction company. We had a few employees and several jobs, mostly remodels and energy upgrades. The young man came to see me one day looking for a fill-in job, before he started his own construction company building homes here in Sitka. Before I asked him about his qualifications, I told him we were replacing lots of windows, and adding insulation and ventilation to several homes under energy upgrade program administered by the State. I said, "If you take the job, one day you might be helping replace a window, the next you might be in an attic adding insulation, and next you might be crawling on your belly to access an area in a crawlspace that needs insulating." He responded, "I'm a college graduate and an expert in new home construction. I don't crawl in dirty crawlspaces!" I countered, "An expert, ha? What did you do working with your dad? Did you do foundation work, framing, finish work, roofing? How did you become an expert?" I held my laughter when he said he had done none of the above, but was his dad's Quality Control Agent. Through my laughter I told him, "We don't need a Quality Control Agent. That's my job." Shortly after, he got his Handyman's License and, because he was a nice guy with a couple of cute kids, people took pity on him and gave him small jobs for a couple of years. He talked his out-of-town landlord into letting him do some remodel work in lieu of paying rent. I never saw the work he did in that home, but I was told by a reliable source that a five-year-old with a dull hatchet might have done better work. I was called to fix some of his work, work I turned away. The little of his work I saw wasn't very good. In the end, he failed miserably as a contractor and he ran back home to daddy to once again be an expert Quality Control Agent.

In the medical field there are good, and "just okay" doctors. The best advice I've gotten usually comes from GP's, not the specialists. Exceptions, like Dr. Horan, my pulmonologist at Virginia Mason Hospital in Seattle, not only looks at how my lungs are working, but considers how my whole body is functioning. She is truly an expert in her specialty, and is also very modest, another sign of a real expert.

Other specialists I've seen get so focused on their specialty that they lose the ability to see what else could be causing a problem. The first neurologist at Virginia Mason was convinced Primary Progressive Aphasia caused my voice loss. She didn't look at other possibilities until a more experienced neurologist saw that because my tongue seemed larger than normal, I should be checked for Acromegaly. He was right. I do also have Acromegaly. The first neurologist had recently completed her residency, and hopefully, with more experience, she will become another true expert.

The first ENT [ear nose and throat] specialist I saw is said to be one of the best in the Northwest. That may be true, but she had the bedside manor of an angry porcupine. Is she a true expert? In my opinion she might be, but what good is it if she can't treat humans with a little compassion and respect? We refused to see her a second time, I saw another ENT who was very nice and knew his stuff. He told us that he knows how uncomfortable a nasal endoscope examination of the throat is because monthly he lets students practice on him—the sign of a true expert.

Both times at the Virginia Mason Hospital ER, I've been impressed with the efficiency and professionalism of the staff. These ER nurses and doctors are truly experts at what they do. At least one ER doctor and a nurse saved my life after I had a bad reaction to penicillin. But I'm even more impressed with the GP's that end up being the admitting doctors, and the ones who take care of the patients once they are admitted. These doctors must have extensive knowledge of every malady a person can get. They end up making many diagnoses with the help of others. These doctors subsequently make recommendations for drugs and therapies to help the person recover. This last trip I was especially impressed by a doctor who not only came up with what I'm now sure were the right diagnoses, but asked all the right questions to get me on a drug therapy that has kept my legs pain free at night for the first time in over a year and a half—another true expert.

The two physicians I've primarily dealt with here in Sitka have proven to be experts with wide ranging skills they probably wouldn't have if they practiced medicine in a large city. In a small town in Alaska, doctors need broad medical knowledge to serve the needs of their patients. Dr. Hunter, who has treated me during the last four years, has researched the latest symptoms of both Acromegaly and ALS. Many doctors have only heard of Acromegaly in medical school and have never treated someone with the disease. This is true to a lesser extent with ALS. Dr. Hunter can probably count his Sitka ALS patients on one hand. And, I'm darn sure I'm the only Acromegaly patient he's ever had. My maladies have forced him to become a bit of an expert in the care and treatment of both of these rare diseases.

Then there is Dr. Don Lehmann. I was extra lucky here, because I got to know him when we built his and his wife's retirement dream home. I first met Don when we came to Sitka and I went in for an annual physical. I liked him right away. Shortly, after our grandson Blake fell off his bike and hit his nose on sharp rock. That rock literally cut the end of Blake's nose off and left it hanging by just the faintest piece of skin. At the ER, Dr. Hunter took one look at Blake's nose and called Dr. Lehmann. Don, who had worked Bethel, Alaska, had repaired lots of lacerations from dog bites, and sewed Blake's nose back on. Now you have to look closely to see the scar. Later, I learned that Don is a well-respected sports doctor, is certified to do cesarean sections, and assist orthopedic surgeons with knee surgery among other specialties. He's a well-rounded expert in the needs of Alaska medicine.

I'm using a wheelchair given to us by the Evergreen ALS Association Chapter. Per a recommendation, we promised to have it adjusted by an expert. So, I promised him we would. The physical therapist we were referred to saw us for a pre-appointment visit. He looked at the chair for a couple of minutes, told us to make an appointment during which he'd adjust the chair. At this appointment the PT said he didn't have any tools. He mostly sat on the floor looking at the chair scratching his head and telling us about how he adjusted mountain bikes all the time. When I said we'd make the adjustments, he asked us to make another appointment so that he could see what we did. He had a couple of good suggestions, but his lack of professionalism truncated our relationship. Like so many things in life, if you want it done right, do it yourself.

I don't claim to be an expert at anything. But I always tried my best at my work. I wasn't afraid to admit when I didn't know something, and was always willing to learn to build my skill base. And I never said I could do something without first having the tools to do the job. What "expert" would say they could do a job, and then not have the correct tools? No expert I know.

Green Beanies & Gurus

3/29/18

The other night I was thinking about how fortunate I am. I might have ALS, but many who are stricken with the disease have it much worse than me. The timing when it hits their lives is far worse than I can imagine. I follow several Facebook sites and some blog posts of others with ALS, and, some stories, especially those of young people with young families, make me cry. One young woman, who lives half way around the world from me, has a very cute little boy who is less than two years old. I tear up every time I read her posts. Another young man who lives a third of the way around the world has two beautiful young daughters. That, too, makes me very sad. As sad as those stories are, they at least have family members who can help and support them. Another young woman on the east coast of the US is totally on her own. She rode a bus to and from the hospital to have a PEG feeding tube installed with no one to help her. That is extra sad to me; I'm fortunate.

As I lay there I thought about how grateful I am for my family, especially my wife. In 1972 when I was a senior in high school, who could have ever guessed I'd be smart enough to recognize that the cute girl in my drama class was the right woman for me to spend my life with? That was the best decision of my life. There hasn't been a day in all those years that I haven't recognized how lucky I am to have Connie as my best friend and wife.

Statistics say most young marriages don't last. And I've been asked more than once for the secret is to our long marriage. The answer, in all honesty, is Connie. But when pressed, I'd say love, family, commitment, compromise, respect, play, shared interests, laughter, humor and silliness. Not foolish silliness, but fun silliness. Just like it's impossible to panic if you keep your breathing under control, it's impossible to stay mad if you look at the silliness and humor in actions that lead to anger. Like most negative actions, anger leads to self-destruction, unhappiness and a downward spiral. Humor and silliness are two of the best ways to squelch the anger.

I no longer remember how these two silly long-standing traditions got started. For many years when Connie made a good dinner, baked something good, or did anything wonderful, I'd tell her, "You get a green beanie for that." Once I told her that a blue ribbon might be the highest honor at the country fair, but in my world, a higher award is the "Green Beanie." Connie has earned at least one "Green Beanie" every day since I learned I have ALS.

I've also told Connie I could sell her to some Gurus because she is so valuable as the perfect example of what a person should be. The gurus could put her up on a pedestal and softly chant "Connie, Connie," to reach the perfect state of nirvana. Pure silliness, but it's also another way of saying, "I love you," without sounding like broken record.

Connie made a very tasty casserole for lunch recently with friends, and that same night, made bread dough for cinnamon rolls for yesterday's breakfast. All this on top of her daily chores, the chores that I used to do and taking care of me. I typed into my phone that she had earned a couple of "Green Beanies," and that I was darn glad I never sold her to the gurus. Pure silliness, and not ashamed of it. The secret to a long marriage is to stay happy with the person you chose to be your mate. If it takes silliness and humor to do that, go for it.

It's the same when dealing with ALS, or any demoralizing disease. When the gloominess starts to creep in, try to see some humor and try to be silly. Connie continues to win more and more "Green Beanie" awards. She would probably have been better off selling me to perhaps, the rendering plant?

Physical Therapy [PT]

3/20/18

MEMO TO: Those who consider Physical Therapy for their ALS patients

FROM: Marcel LaPerriere

DATE: March 2018

Physical therapy is controversial with ALS patients. A trip to the Emergency Room at Virginia Mason Hospital, two days in that hospital, tons of blood tests, and talking to several doctors convinced me that physical therapy was bad for me.

About two weeks after I started physical therapy, I went for my morning walk. I felt good, so I sat down for about an hour. Then I did squats with the ball against the wall, and toe lifts; about five more repetitions than I before, because it felt fine; no pain. And after all, I should have been getting stronger. I then sat down for a couple of hours work on the computer, simultaneously doing the ankle exercises.

After the walk, and for sure after the squats, I should have lain down and elevated my legs. By late afternoon both legs were swelling, and by the next morning my left leg was both swollen and very painful. I could hardly walk. In a couple of days, I went to see Dr. Hunter suspecting a blood clot. An ultrasound of the left leg showed good news; no blood clot.

About a week later the leg started feeling good enough that I could start walking again. After two weeks, shortly before we went to Seattle for medical appointments, it felt good enough that I restarted the physical therapy exercises. About two days before we left, I walked, then did the physical therapy. Big mistake. Again, swelling and pain was exacerbated by not lying down to elevate my legs.

On the 25th of February we flew south to Seattle. This involves lots of sitting, followed by lots of walking to just get out of the Seattle Airport. We took an Uber to the hotel near Virginia Mason, and by the time we got there both legs were very swollen. My feet were so swollen, my tennis shoes had to be unlaced as far as they could be. On the 27th I could hardly walk, and the swelling was as bad as ever. When I saw my pulmonologist that day, she, too, suspected blood clots, and ordered blood tests The results showed an elevated D Dimmer, high white count and low red count. Another ultrasound on both legs showed no blood clots.

The next day I had a continuous four-and-a-half-hour ALS Clinic, where I saw every ALS specialist under the sun. The last doctor I saw was the ALS neurologist. She of course, had to do a complete range of motion on me and check reflexes. At the end of that exam the swelling was unreal, and the pain was excruciatingly off the scale. I could no longer walk with the walker and went into a mild shock. Soon I was in the ER.

After many more blood tests and being seen by who knows how many doctors, their conclusion was that as ALS advances, the skeletal muscle pump is compromised and therefore the heart can no longer pump the blood back up from the legs. This causes not only swelling of the soft tissue, but it also causes periostitis (inflammation of the periosteum.) When I was exercising, what is left of my leg muscles was calling for extra blood, especially when doing the squats.

After being admitted to the hospital I was given an IV of Lasix, and over a period of four to six hours, I urinated off over four liters of urine. You could literally see the swelling go down. After that shock to my system I found walking nearly impossible. Hence the wheelchair. I've gotten a little better in the last couple of weeks, but I can no longer walk more than a few feet with the walker.

I now know that I should have elevated my legs after exercising. Icing would have made the situation worse, and the hospital personnel kept warm blankets on my legs to keep the fluids at the lowest viscosity as possible.

I think physical therapy for an ALS patient early on is good. But, as the disease progresses I think exercise does more harm than good.

One reason I kept walking as long as I did was that I walked every day. Losing my ability to walk was inevitable. That loss just came a couple of months earlier than it might have I had known what I do now.

Thank you for listening.

PEG Feeding Tube

3/21/18

Everything you wanted to know but were afraid to ask...

My ignorance could still fill volumes but I'm learning to live with a Percutaneous Endoscopic Gastrostomy (PEG) feeding tube.

I still eat mostly by mouth, but about half my liquid per day comes though the PEG. Drinking liquids with the viscosity of water can be hard. For over a year I've only been able to sip water and other thin liquids. Thus, to get enough hydration I depend on moist foods. I also sip on water or apple juice pretty much all day. Even, with that, it's been hard to get the liquid I need. Hence the PEG.

As ALS progresses constipation can become a real problem. Decreased activity, a compromised diaphragm muscle, and some medications are the primary causes of constipation. Other muscles that aid digestion also diminish in function. And being dehydrated doesn't help.

I was always a "regular sort of guy," but now, constipation is not only darned uncomfortable, but can be very serious. Using the PEG, I increase my hydration level, including a half-cup of prune juice every day. Not having to endure the gawd awful taste of the juice, while getting its benefits has turned out to be a big plus.

I've also been experimenting with liquid food. A Virginia Mason Hospital dietician gave us a recommendation for a full-time 2850-calorie per day diet of liquid food—not much fun. Why so many calories? Because of the diminished ability to digest food? To get that many calories I'd need six cans a day. Each can takes about 15 minutes to empty, so that would mean Connie would be feeding me an hour and half a day—crazy. After little more than a half can, I get a sort of blood sugar high and get woozy. We tried a bottle of Ensure, but I passed out after about six ounces. Connie says I was still talking, but was white as a sheet. I have no recollection of the conversation, but she says I looked dazed for a couple of minutes. To minimize the dizziness, I must have something in my stomach when we start the liquid food, and Connie must slowly inject the food.

The PEG leaks a little, and the discharge has an interesting sweet smell—somewhat like the breath of a baby who is only eating milk—weird. I found out the hard way not to bump the PEG too hard. The other night I woke myself up by accidentally bumping it with my hand; it hurt like crazy. Maybe it will become less sensitive as my belly heals from the surgery. It's also sensitive to cold, so I need to dress warmly if I go outside on a cold day. When Connie pushes me in the wheelchair it feels weird each time we hit an expansion crack in the sidewalk.

I'm sure the PEG will continue to educate us. Meanwhile it gives us some amusement. Just this morning the syringe nearly slipped out of the tube that I was holding at eye level. I laughed as I envisioned spraying my face with a full syringe of food. Good thing my glasses are safety glasses. Maybe I need to wear my old hard hat, too. One never knows when a wayward syringe of volatile Two Cal HN calorie and protein dense nutrition will go astray—especially in the hands of an out of control, laughing caregiver.

Gadgets, Stuff and Things

3/24/18

I'm amazed at how many gadgets, things and stuff it takes to live with ALS. A short list of some things that I'm now dependent on follows:

Hospital bed. Many healthcare professionals were right when they said I'd breathe better when sleeping if my head was elevated. The back of the bed lifts to help my night breathing and in the morning, to help me sit up. Elevating my feet reduces swelling. It's easier to get into and out of because it's higher than a standard bed. Connie replaced the trapeze that hung from a frame with a nice webbing sling I use to pull myself into sitting position. Also new to me is an electric blanket. Because the blood circulation in my legs and feet is so poor, a half a dozen standard blankets weren't enough to keep my legs and feet warm. I love that the electric blanket solved that problem and am finding the heat is a very comfortable way to sleep.

The BIPAP machine sits on the bed stand and helps me breathe when sleeping. It requires distilled water for its reservoir to moisten the air, and also takes special unscented baby wipes to clean the mask each morning.

Though I hate that I must use it, the wheelchair that the ALS Association gave me is working out wonderfully. It's comfortable, and I can reach most of the things I need from it. It fits under my desk, so I can sit at my computer easily. Its wheels are now my access to the outside world. And our dog, Bella, and I have a new game. I toss one of her toys across the room and then we race to see who can get to it first. She always wins, but it's fun for both of us.

The walker. With it, I can walk from the bed to the bathroom. In the bathroom I depend on six different grab bars, and a raised toilet seat with grab bars on its sides. In the shower I have a special seat and use the hand-held shower to bathe.

My iPhone and an app. Since I can't talk, I depend on these to communicate. My iPhone is seldom more than an arm's length away from me, most always in my breast pocket. Since eating takes so long—typically, an hour just for breakfast—I use my iPhone to check the news, Facebook and listen to podcast while I slowly eat. I've become addicted to my phone and it would be darned hard to give it up.

A medium-sized stainless steel bowl, a covered cup of water, and a time-release medication. These sit on the kitchen counter, and the bowl holds all the paraphernalia for my feeding tube. The water is warming to room temperature in preparation for injection through my feeding tube. One doesn't want to inject ice-cold filtered water from the fridge. I'm supposed to take the time-release medication about a half hour before breakfast without food, but I can't swallow it without a spoon full of applesauce. Because it's a time-release medication, it can't be crushed and pushed through the feeding tube with water. It could be cut open, mixed with something like applesauce, and administered via the feeding tube, but it's just easier to swallow it.

A nebulizer, a blood pressure machine and a blood oxygen sensor. These machines, plus three different medications I take with either applesauce or ice cream just before bed are at my computer desk. All the other medicines, vitamins and supplements I take with meals are on the dining table.

The last time I depended on this much stuff was when I was scuba diving, caving or climbing—fun adventures. This is my new adventure and I'm happy all of these gadgets, stuff and things are around to make life easier and more enjoyable.

Augie

3/26/18

My biggest takeaway from the movie, *Augie*, is that it pays to be rich if you fall victim to a disease like ALS.

Augustine L. "Augie" Nieto II is the founder and retired chief executive of Life Fitness, as well as the current chairman of theALS Therapy Development Institute. I applaud Augie Nieto for raising millions for ALS research. I wonder if he would have done anything positive with his money had he not been afflicted with ALS? Pre-ALS, Augie doesn't sound like the kind of guy I would have wanted to know. But, like any debilitating disease, ALS has a way of waking a person up to some tough life realities.

I also wonder why the movie had to include so many off color and inappropriate dirty jokes. When I posed this question to Connie, she answered, "That reflects what kind of man he is." In this day of the "Me too" movement it seemed way off base.

I hope Augie continues to raise money for ALS research, lives many more years in his multimillion-dollar house with his four full-time paid caregivers, and can enjoy many more sunsets from the deck of his multimillion dollar yacht.

Recovery?

3/27/18

Even I've been surprised at how much muscle strength I've gained back as I recover from our epic Seattle trip. This morning I was able to mostly stand in the shower. I couldn't have done that just two weeks ago. And, I'm even taking a couple of steps without the walker. Wow! Is some of the strength returning because I take steroids for a breathing problem? I don't know the answers.

One of the most liberating things about getting a bit stronger and having a bit more mobility is I can dress myself. Two weeks ago I couldn't change my own socks, put on my own underwear or pants. It might seem like a silly thing to celebrate, but to me it's big. How long will it last? I have no idea, but I'll take every day of it.

It's funny how the little things in life I used to take for granted can now give me such joy. Either way, I'll continue loving the life of living with the woman I love and our cute little dog that daily makes me happy. ALS sucks, but life is good.

Medications

3/28/18

I was the kind of guy who never even took an aspirin, and I'd literally go years without any medications crossing my lips. Additionally, illegal drugs, even pot, were not for me. Today though, I depend on several drugs.

First, a 10mg Omeprazole capsule helps control heartburn by reducing stomach acid. Some literature about ALS and many doctors say ALS does not cause excessive heartburn. If all the throat muscles and the esophagus sphincter muscles are improperly working, how can you say ALS does not contribute to heartburn? A physician at a Virginia Mason ALS Clinic I visited specializes in medications, and had seen enough ALS patients to know that ALS can exacerbate heartburn. Since I started the Omeprazole nearly a month ago, I have had zero heartburn. Before, I took over a dozen antacids a day. ALS certainly contributed to my heartburn, and I'm thankful for the ALS doctor who realized it.

A daily puff of Breo Ellipta helps with my breathing. Ten days ago I was having some real issues with breathing, so my GP prescribed 10mg of Prednisone with breakfast and dinner. It appears I need 10 to 14 days of Prednisone every two to three months. I wish the long-term side effects of Prednisone weren't so bad, because when I'm taking it, I have more energy and strength. Both my pulmonologist and ALS doctor say I should minimize the use of Prednisone, as it can mask a less serious problem that could build into pneumonia. I'll take it only when I need it.

Ten years ago and pre-ALS I developed high blood pressure, and started taking 40mg Lisinopril daily. When just 20 mg of Lisinopril gave me a persistent cough, I changed to 50mg Losartan, with food every night. Losartan causes sleepiness, so I now take it in the evening.

Between 7:30 to 8:00 p.m. I take 10mg Baclofen to lessen muscle cramps, 300mg Gabapentin to treat neuropathic pain, and 25mg Mirabegron which helps the bladder muscles relax. Baclofen and the Gabapentin work together, and since I've used that combo, I've had no leg muscle cramps or the associated pain. Before, I would have several leg cramps per night. Thanks to the Virginia Mason GP for coming up with the Baclofen and Gabapentin combination that lets me sleep though the night cramp-free.

Occasionally I use an Albuterol inhaler to relieve the asthma symptoms. I usually take three or four puffs instead of the prescribed two, because ALS prevents me from holding my breath, as directed. If after 30 minutes the asthma symptoms remain, I use the nebulizer with Albuterol. The nebulizer is equivalent to around seven puffs from an Albuterol inhaler, so it normally does the trick. I hate using it, though, because it leaves me light headed and makes my hands shake.

I basically hate pharmaceutical companies. The drugs they have developed help millions of people around the world, but they have profited by over-manufacturing and promoting drug over-usage. The opioid crisis is a very complex issue but I think painkiller manufacturers are the main culprits. They knew damn well they were making more pills than there was a legitimate demand for, and lobbied Congress to keep the Drug Enforcement Agency (DEA) from regulating the production, policing the distribution or taking any other measures that could have prevented this very costly epidemic. They did this to raise their profits and pay a few upper managers way more than anyone should ever be paid. The drugs they produce have done many people a lot of good, including me. I just wish they could operate with a more altruistic goal and less of a profit motive.

Reflection and Joy

3/30/18

As ALS continues to rob me of abilities and traps me more and more within my own body, I have lots of time to reflect on the past. Though there are plenty of bad memories of hardships, dwelling on bad times is unhealthy. I focus on memories of life-building experiences and times of joy. Thoughts of positive interactions with people, and happy occasions are a good way to fight off the blues.

How to fight depression? Bring some joy into your life; past and present. I recall the births of my son and three grandsons and the joys of family. In nearly 46 years of marriage we have had many hard times, with struggles that often seemed insurmountable. Knowing we stayed strong and overcame those obstacles brings me joy.

I spend much of my day sitting at my computer since I can't talk, and am mostly confined to a wheelchair. Social media allows social contact with other humans. I'm grateful to live in a time when technology makes it possible for me to make cyber-friends all over the world. That brings me joy.

Writing about some of the people who have made me the person I am is rewarding. Three men, my older brother Fred, a Jesuit Catholic Priest named Fr. Federer and my high school drama teacher Mr. Larson were positive role models when I was a teenager. Remembering the good times I had with those great men has brought me happiness. Writing about them, too, has been good therapy, and the joy from that simple action has pushed any undesirable thoughts far away.

I seek joy in bright things in my daily life. This morning I awoke in my hospital–type bed that sits alongside my wife Connie's bed. Our little beagle, Bella, was snuggled next to Connie, and I smiled. When I hear Connie gently snoring away in unison with Bella in the middle of the night, I smile. Life is too full of joy to stay depressed by this terrible disease. I hate ALS, but I'm happy to say I'm still in love with life.

Wobbly

4/7/18

In the mid '70s when our son Zach was learning to walk, he'd say in his cute little voice, "wobbly" as he stood or took a step. He probably learned that word because we'd play with his egg shaped Weeble toys; their sales slogan was "They wobble, but don't fall down." To us, he was our little Weeble, and like all toddlers, he was wobbly on his feet.

Getting out of the shower this morning, holding one of several grab bars, I thought of how wobbly I am on my feet. I've lost so much muscle mass in my legs and arms, my bulk is all midsection now, I'm a bit egg shaped. Maybe I'm now a living Weeble? I haven't fallen so far, so like a Weeble; I'm wobbly, but don't fall down.

I recently read of an ALS victim who can still walk, talk and eat, but can't move her arms. That means she can't feed herself, get dressed, bathe or use the toilet alone. Not being able to brush her hair is what she missed most. Initially, I thought she'd miss eating, or maybe being able to dress herself. But later, it made sense. One's hair is the sign we put out to the public to say who we are. ALS has robbed her of the ability to do that. I'm lucky I can still do things most people take for granted, like bathing and dressing myself.

It's okay that I can't talk, have a wheel chair and have turned into a wobbly Weeble. I can still use my arms, and I'm grateful for that.

Suicide

4/10/18

Talking about suicide is painful, controversial, and darn scary for some.

Most people, when diagnosed with a degenerative disease like ALS, contemplate suicide. I have. Not because I can't face what's coming, but because I don't want to burden others. What keeps me from taking a full bottle of pills, jumping off the O'Connell Bridge or enacting any other means of committing suicide? The short answer is twofold. First, suicide is devastatingly painful for the survivors, and second, as much as I hate ALS, I'm happy and I'm enjoying life.

More than forty years ago a good friend committed suicide. It was painful for me then, and I still wonder if I could have done something to prevent his premature death. Few things haunt a family more than a suicide; it spreads immense pain throughout the family and friends. The pain a family suffers after a suicide can be worse than watching a loved one die from a cruel disease like ALS. So, as bad as ALS is likely to get for me, I can't see taking the suicide solution. It would hurt my family. Worse than becoming dependent on others, is bestowing that kind of pain on loved ones.

Physician-assisted suicide helps terminally ill people end their lives with dignity. I totally support it in the five states and District of Columbia where it's legal and think it should be an option in all 50 states. I wrote our state legislators a couple of years ago supporting a physician-assisted suicide law here in Alaska. One of Connie's elderly great aunts had taken an old cat into the vet to be put asleep. She told Connie, "The cat just peacefully went to sleep, so why can't I do the same?" That's a fair question for terminally ill people, and I think they should have that option.

Connie says she would rather have me be a burden on her, than not be here. That's comforting to me, because as I write this she is in our basement cleaning my old woodshop. I should be led out at dawn, blindfolded and placed before a firing squad for leaving that 10-year-old mess for her. If she doesn't kill me, or even yell at me for leaving the mess, she must be serious about having me around. Humm… maybe she loves me as much as I love her. There will be no suicide in my future. I couldn't do that to her or the rest of my family.

Bedsore

4/12/18

This morning Connie and I found that I have a stage-1 bedsore on my left heel. Two nights ago the heel was a little sore. But after five straight hours of sleep last night, very unusual for me, my heel was extra sore.

Online research and photos of bedsores and their progression brought us wide awake to their danger. Lowering the hospital bed flat from time to time is as important as raising its head and foot. When it's flat, I can roll onto my side. As hard as it is to roll, I need to make the effort to prevent bedsores.

Forty years ago I dislocated my right knee, and have had a pronated right leg ever since. That's why my right heel isn't also showing signs of a bedsore. I start the night lying with my right foot straight up, but as the night wears on, because of the pronated leg, it rotates outward. And, that movement is keeping the right heel bedsore free. Who would have guessed an old injury could be beneficial?

Several have correctly warned me about bedsores. A stage-1 bedsore is more than enough. I'll take preventative measures before it gets any worse.

Overdoing It

4/15/18

Saturday morning dawned clear and warm, so Connie and I drove to the Sea-walk. From the boardwalk covered breakwater we can sit in the sun and watch people, animals and boats. Boats always interest our little dog Bella. She knows it takes a boat to go to Whale Island, her favorite place on earth where two of her dog friends live. We saw several sea lions, probably feeding on herring, because swarms of seagulls circled and dove for scraps. Bella jumped down on the rocks to sniff for minks. I love this excursion, but it's a bit of a workout for me. When I was walking, I never noticed the slight hills to the observation area on the breakwater. Now it takes my all to get up those hills, and the hill to get to the truck is the worst of all.

After a quick stop at the Backdoor Bakery, we headed home. As we drove I asked Connie by typing into my phone to grab a chunk of firewood that I'd seen in the firewood shed to build a paper towel holder for the bathroom. Since cutting the wood was going to require a tricky cut on the chop saw, I'd have to make my way downstairs to the wood shop. I also wanted to see Connie's cleaning job.

When we got home we enjoyed our bakery goodies. Maybe it was the reheated coffee that made me feel energetic enough to go down the stairs, or maybe it was pure insanity. I'm not sure which, but it wasn't a good idea.

I rolled my wheelchair to the edge of the stairs, and then started inching my way down. My legs are no longer strong enough to navigate stairs, so I stood sideways holding the railings with both hands. Fortunately, the stairs to the shop are not as steep as our inside stairs, and there is a large landing half way down where I could rest. I'm guessing it took me four to five minutes to get down the stairs. Once there, I made my way to the chop saw that sits just outside the wood shop, and made the tricky cuts. Then it was time to see Connie's cleaning progress. I can no longer lift my legs the twenty inches to step over the foundation to get into the shop, so Connie lifted my legs one at a time, and I navigated to a stool. Not surprisingly, she has done an amazing job cleaning up years of accumulated sawdust and organizing the tools. Soon it was time to make my way back up the stairs. I think it took twice as long to get up the stairs than down. I literally had to pull myself up the stairs with my arms, and rested to catch my breath, a few times, as well. Once on the main floor I went directly into the bedroom and I took an hour-long nap. Connie sanded and urethaned the new paper towel holder.

After my nap I got up for lunch and noted that both of my legs were sore, and worse, were swelling like crazy. That meant I needed to get them elevated, so after lunch I took another hour-long nap. The elevating didn't do the trick and both legs continued to swell. By late afternoon my left leg had swollen about 20% normal size, and my right leg and foot had swollen about 50 to 60% over normal size. My right foot looked like someone had placed an air hose into it and inflated it like a balloon. It was puffed up with four normal sized toes sticking out, and a big toe that was also about 50% oversized. Worse, my right ankle felt like it had a bad sprain. I could no longer stand on it, even when holding onto something.

When our almost eight-year-old grandson Lucky was coming to stay the night about 5:00, my right leg was throbbing and fairly painful. I had to lie down and elevate that leg, which made it harder for me to enjoy having Lucky at our house. After dinner, even though it was only 6:30, I had to go to bed. Lucky wanted to play with the slot cars that are upstairs, so I didn't feel as guilty as I would have otherwise.

I got up this morning at 6:00 a.m., and even with all that sleep I still felt tired. My left leg was back to normal size and my right leg was only about 20% oversized. My right ankle still felt sprained, but I could again stand and walk short distances with my walker.

At the ALS Clinic in February the pulmonologist quoted others saying, "It's all about energy conservation." My version: "It's all about energy management."

Clearly, I over did it, and this side of an emergency, I don't see myself braving the stairs again. In March I said stairs were now out of the question for me. That was true for upstairs. I have gone downstairs twice since then. Now I can safely say, never again. It was rewarding to be creative and use my hands to actually build something, but the price I paid wasn't worth it.

I'm happy with the paper towel holder, which I mounted low enough to reach from my wheelchair. One symptom of Bulbar Onset ALS is perpetual drooling. I never want to be without something to wipe my mouth. I'm as bad as a little baby when it comes to drooling, but that's okay with me. I've always loved babies, and am not ashamed to join their ranks—so long as I have something to wipe the slobber off my beard.

CRISPR

4/18/18

CRISPR, pronounced "crisper," stands for Clustered Regularly Interspaced Short Palindromic Repeats, a tool used to edit part of the genome. It's very complicated, but from what I read and what I've heard on podcasts, it might be the current most promising tool for preventing, and possibly curing, some genetic and possibly even non-genetic diseases.

As I understand it, CRISPR finds a genetically defective gene, and has the potential to repair it. It may be able to remove a gene and replace it with another one. Now being tested in the treatment of cancer patients, it's still too early to say if CRISPR treatments are successful.

Researchers have also started using CRISPR to potentially treat ALS. So far it has shown promising results in lab mice. I know of no testing on humans, but word is, if there is a bright spot on the horizon for the treatment of ALS, it is CRISPR.

I read this morning that CRISPR helped isolate TP73 as one of the 15 genes, of around 20,000, that are in some way responsible for sporadic (non-hereditary) ALS. Variations in the TP73 gene could be one the causes of ALS. The article didn't say if CRISPR could repair that gene. Other sources report a high probability that CRISPR could be used to fix the broken part of that gene. If the TP73 gene is repaired, will the progression of ALS be halted? Or, even reversed?

There might be a dark side to CRISPR too. Generally speaking, CRISPR is showing the potential to cure many diseases. Scientists in China were the first to edit genes in human embryos, and the same editing techniques using CRISPR has now been done in the U.S. This poses many questions regarding the ethics of engineering humans. Are we playing God when we start altering embryos? What if some future Hitler decides to use CRISPR to engineer the perfect fighting soldier? Or, uses CRISPR to alter genes of soldiers? CRISPR could be used to make soldiers more aggressive and tolerant of pain. What if a future Hitler used CRISPR to build an Aryan race? Should the world put limitations on CRISPR uses? Do we humans have the right to play God? I see no harm in preventing or curing diseases, but I do have ethical concerns about engineering humans.

Guano Happens

4/20/18

When Connie and I were doing a lot of caving, a bumper sticker on our truck said "GUANO HAPPENS," and at the end of the lettering was the silhouette of a bat flying out of a cave. Of course, the "guano happens" was a play on words, and it always surprised me when people didn't understand the bumper sticker. People often asked, "What's guano?" and when I explained that it was bat droppings, most got the joke. I say joke; but I firmly espouse to the philosophy that "shit happens." We may not like it, but there are things that are out of our control. Guano happens, and we need to learn to deal with it and make the best of each situation.

Connie, good friends Tom and Juby, (yes, the name is spelled J-u-b-y) and I have shared many adventures, including some when guano happened. One year towards the end of September we were boating in our 45-foot, custom-built sailing schooner, Terra Nova, around Prince of Whales Island in Southeast Alaska. We had been anchored in a shallow bay for a couple of days while Tom, Connie and I explored a few caves. Since autumn can be stormy and since the bay was so shallow, we put out bow and stern anchors to keep us from drifting into even shallower water. The third night around 10:00 shortly after we went to bed, we heard a clunk. Connie got up to check the depth sounder and it showed we still had plenty of water under our keel.

We had set an alarm to go off if the water got less than a fathom (less than six feet) of water under our keel. Since all looked okay, we went back to sleep. Less than a half-hour later, though, the dishes we'd left in the dish drainer started to slide and crash into the sink. The boat was listing to port. You guessed it; we had hit bottom. But the depth sounder still showed plenty of water below our keel, and we'd been anchored in the same place the two previous nights. Plus, the tides were no lower than they had been—so what was happening? The boat was listing more and more as the tide continued to go out, and we all realized we'd just have to wait a few hours for the tide to come back in. And we weren't going to get any sleep. Guano happens, and we were going to have to deal with it.

I got the dingy out of the davits and lowered into the water. Connie made hot tea and soon, we were all in the dingy, headed for the beach in near total darkness. We started a large fire and enjoyed tea with cookies. I had left the running lights on the boat, so we could see that the boat listed until it reached about 45 degrees. There was nothing we could do to help the boat, so we enjoyed the fire and waited with our friends. Connie and I were a bit worried because the boat was not only our home, but expensive. After about four hours on the beach, nearly 3:00 in the morning, Terra Nova was floating free again, and we could go back to bed. Even though guano had happened, we'd faced it and made the best of it. The next day I dove under the boat and found one very large boulder on the bottom. The two previous nights we must have missed it by just a few feet, but the third night the front of the keel sat firmly planted on the boulder. The depth sounder was positioned such that the boulder didn't show; only the deeper water in front of if was being sounded.

What does "guano happens" have to do with ALS?

If ALS has taught me nothing else, it has taught me life isn't always fair. Some ALS patients have an extremely hard time coping with the disease. I've struggled from time to time myself, and I'm lucky that my ALS hasn't been more aggressive. But I realize that guano happens, and I need to make the best of it. Some people would rather play the "blame game" than admit that life isn't always fair; that guano happens.

Not long ago a man posted on Facebook blaming the government for the recent death of his dad who had ALS. This poor man was grieving, and was very angry. I understand that totally. In the post he claimed the government had a cure for ALS but would not release it because it would be too expensive. That's just crazy. It would cost less for the government to release a cure if they had it. And ALS research is ongoing in the US, China, Russia, India, Japan, The Netherlands, Britain, France, Spain, Germany, Australia, New Zealand and other countries. If one government suppresses a cure, wouldn't that mean that these other countries agreed to suppress it, as well? Even crazier, within a day of his post over a dozen people said they agreed with him 100%.

Another person posted that three adult siblings were fighting over who should take care of their dad who was suffering from ALS. Each thought it wasn't fair that they would have to care for their father, whom they claimed they loved. All three had their own kids, their own jobs and their own houses. The fight was tearing the family apart, and saddest of all, it was placing guilt and blame on the father. He didn't ask to get ALS, yet the family feud between his children was adding to his misery. I'd tell the three siblings to grow up and that life isn't always fair. Guano happens and the responsible thing to do is make the best of it. Fighting makes it harder for all concerned.

During the boat trip mentioned above, Juby came up with the saying, "Guano often happens at night." She also said, "Frequently, guano happens to good people." The latter made me recall an online article I read shortly after I was diagnosed with ALS. Written by a nurse who had spent thirty some years caring for ALS patients, she said it seemed that it was always the nicest people who seemed to get ALS. In a strange twist of fate when she was about to retire, she was diagnosed with ALS. Guano can be especially cruel. The article made my heart bleed for the poor woman. She had spent her adult life caring for and seeing the effects of ALS, only to have to face the end of her life dealing with the ravages of the disease. What impressed me—she held her head high. And in a polite way, she said she knew that shit happens.

In our 46 years together Connie and I have face our fare share of guano. Some was self-inflected, some just happened, and some got dumped on us. I'm proud that we have always faced the guano head on and have never fought over the adversity or played the "blame game." Early 20th Century humorist Will Rogers said, "If you find yourself in a hole, stop digging." ALS is the biggest bit of guano we've ever had to face. We'd be pure fools to do any more than shovel the shit out of our way, and digging deeper would be crazy.

Worthless

4/28/18

The ALS Monster is good at taking away abilities while giving its victims feelings of worthlessness. The more it takes more away, the more dependent on others one becomes. If one can't help with the day-to-day chores or the family income, one must feel worthless? I get that feeling from time to time.

But I will fight the ALS Monster as long as I can; that's one of the reasons I write. I may not be the best writer, but hopefully I can help others while helping myself deal with ALS. Maybe I can help others ward off depression and other negative thoughts through my writing? Maybe my writing will help caregivers, and elicit more empathy for ALS victims? Maybe some will understand that we victims of ALS, like most victims of any atrocity, didn't ask for the hand we've been dealt. None of us are asking for sympathy, all we want is understanding.

As humans, there are few feelings as detrimental as worthlessness. Being loved and needed are near the top of the human emotional needs pyramid. We all want to contribute to our family and society. ALS robs us of so much, especially in the latter stages; it's hard to see that we still have value. Will our loved ones mourn and miss us when we are gone? Yes. What if we lose the ability to move? Are we not still parents, grandparents, brothers, sisters, children, grandchildren, aunts and uncles? Yes. Therefore we still have value.

A friend and former employee disappeared at sea, and is presumed drowned. Sadder still, he and his 24-year-old daughter never met. Yet the bond between them remains, and she is greatly mourning the loss of her father. At his memorial no one was crying harder than she was. The invisible strings that bind families together are stronger than we might guess, and that bond gives each of us value.

ALS first robbed me of my ability to talk, but I could still walk and be active. When I couldn't talk, I shut my construction company down. When ALS started taking away my balance and breathing became harder and harder, even easy tasks fatigued me, which made it even harder to do construction work. Some home chores that I had done in the past became impossible. When ALS took away my ability to walk and forced me into a wheelchair, I felt even more worthless. I will not give into the ALS Monster. But being able to write has helped, and I'm grateful that I still have the use of my arms.

Despite the fact I can't talk, a local nonprofit group lets me do some volunteer work. I'm part of a Building Committee that has been making recommendations on the remodel of a historic building that is the headquarters for the nonprofit group. Last week I spent several hours looking over sixty some pages of prints on my computer. It felt good to be doing something productive and feel like I had some value.

This past week my sister has been visiting from Colorado. I must have some value as a brother or she wouldn't have taken the time or spent the money to come to Alaska. I'm no longer able to do many of the things around the house that I use to do, my wife has had to take up the slack. Though the ALS continues to deplete my capabilities and I become more of a burden, she still wants me alive. I'm no longer the husband I was, but I have value to the woman who loves me, and that makes me happy.

We victims of ALS need to look at the value we still have, and not concentrate on what we can no longer do. Even if I'm not as much fun for my grandsons as I use to be, they still want to come visit me. I still have some value as a grandfather, and that makes me especially happy.

As long as I'm still kicking, I'm going to fight the ALS Monster. As it takes more from me, I refuse to feel bitterness or worthlessness. It's trying hard to make me feel worthless, but I won't let it. I'll laugh, perhaps not physically, in the face of the Monster each time it tells me I'm worthless, and until I breathe my last breath, I still have value.

Why

5/1/18

The first question most of us who are diagnosed with ALS have is, "Why me?" After some time passes, we replace that question with, "Why?" or, "How come?" What we might have done in our past that triggered the neurological disorder that caused us to become victims of ALS?

The five to 10% of ALS victims who have Familial ALS, caused by heredity, know why. But, why does one family member get ALS, while their sibling doesn't? What turns on the gene that initiates the development of ALS?

Just yesterday an article reported a possible correlation between ALS and diesel exhaust. I've been exposed to not only the exhaust, but I've been soaked to the bone in diesel fuel more times than I'd like to admit. Is my ALS from the dozen years I spent working on very large diesel engines?

Another article suggested that there might be a connection with industrial fertilizer. As a kid, over fifty years ago, I spread a lot of commercial fertilizer and sprayed a lot of pesticides on my father's evergreen nursery. Could that be the cause?

Other articles suggest a possible connection with brain trauma and ALS. Retired NFL Football players have a higher propensity to acquire ALS than the public at large. And military veterans are twice as likely to develop ALS than the general population. Is the propensity for ALS in vets because of brain trauma? I was an abused child with lots of head trauma coming from too many beatings to count. Could that be the cause?

There also appears to be a connection between neurological disorders and heavy metals. I've been exposed to heavy metals for years. As kids we loved to play with mercury; we poured the silvery liquid over our hands. Then there is lead—lead in household paints, melted lead poured into the molds to make fishing weights and lead soldiers, lead in gasoline, white lead lubricant, red lead paint, lead hammers. Even toothpaste used to come in lead tubes. What about all the welding fumes that I breathed over thirty some years of welding that contained tons of heavy metals? Its no surprise that I consider heavy metals might be the culprit.

Like most people with Amyotrophic Lateral Sclerosis, I'll never know what it was that caused my ALS. But I can question why. I can also warn others to be careful when near diesel, chemicals and heavy metals; potential causes. Blake, my 16-year-old grandson, took up blacksmithing and welding when he was about 12. He gets endless lectures from me about long-term exposure to heavy metals and the possible health effects. I'm glad he has listened and always wears a respirator. I'm also glad he is rethinking his long-term career choices and is considering the potential health consequences of those choices. I've told him many times, "I'll never know, but my ALS might be self-inflicted."

Questions like "Why me, why, and how come" are natural questions for anyone whose body malfunctions. Seldom can we answer those nagging questions, but we can use our misfortunes to urge others to protect themselves from potential causes. The questions of "Why and how come" are reasons for a national and possibly worldwide database to start to unravel the mystery of our disease. We need a cure for ALS. And, at least as important is finding how to prevent this horrendous disease. A large database could shed light on commonalities between ALS patients and could show how we could prevent the disease all together. ALS is a rare disease. I say, let's make it even rarer.

Sleep

5/3/18

Connie would tell you one of the things I've always excelled at is sleep. She'd tell you that most nights, ten seconds after my head hit the pillow, I'd be asleep. From time to time as an adult, I have had some difficulty sleeping, but it was rare. For most of my adult life I've had an over-active nighttime bladder, but even after using the restroom, I'd fall right back to sleep. And, I've always made it a point to get a full eight hours of sleep. In short, I love sleeping.

One of the symptoms of ALS is fatigue. Boy, can I relate to that symptom. It feels like I'm always fatigued and tired. And to make things worse, I feel like I haven't done anything to deserve to be fatigued. I'm just always tired for no reason. Except that I have ALS. And, fatigue means, I need sleep— which I do even more of now.

Like all my siblings, I inherited the workaholic gene, and, pre-ALS, ten to twelve-hour workdays were not unusual. When I worked at Sheldon Jackson College as the Director of Maintenance, the job often required 80+ hour workweeks. My normal work day at SJC started at 5:00 a.m., and I almost always worked until 6:00 p.m. Additionally, I frequently got calls in the middle of the night about a broken water pipe or no heat in one of the dorms. When you add the after-hour calls and weekends, that's a lot of hours worked in any given week. During the four years I worked at SJC I never remember being as tired as I now feel most of the time.

As an active scuba diver, diving year round in cold Alaskan waters, I'd often experience what is termed in the diving world, "unearned fatigue." Unearned fatigue is when a body goes into hyperdrive trying to stay warm. Staying warm burns calories like crazy, which causes fatigue. On days when I'd help teach diving, I'd sometimes be in the water for six or more hours. When there were a couple classes back to back, we'd throw in a fun dive. Most classes I helped with were held in the winter, and after that long in the water, I'd come home mighty fatigued. Back then a quick fifteen to thirty-minute nap would restore me to normal. I wish a short nap would restore my energy today.

Now days I go to bed around 8:30 or 9:00 and most days get up around 6:00. Then, I take an hour nap in the morning and an hour nap in the afternoon. Sometimes, I'll toss in another nap. So, I nap up to three hours each day plus sleep around nine hours each night, and still feel tired.

It's a good thing I like to sleep, because I've read that fatigue increases as ALS progresses. Will that mean I'll sleep even more? Probably so. Dogs sleep twelve to fourteen hours a day, so am I entering my dog days? If so, I hope Connie doesn't try to teach me new tricks. They say you can't teach old dogs new tricks and the same goes for old geezers like me.

Hypermetabolism

5/4/18

A new Australian study found on the ALS website shows that some people with ALS have a higher metabolism rate which leads to a more rapid decline and early death. Between 25% to 68% of people that have sporadic ALS like I do will exhibit hypermetabolism, and 100% of Familia ALS patients will have the higher metabolism. This explains why I've had to work so hard to keep weight on for the first three to four years of my ALS. Eating three large meals a day, plus two snacks and a dessert, I'd still lose weight. An extra-large bowl of ice cream several nights each week helped stem the weight loss. Hypermetabolism might also help explain the endless fatigue.

I had lost fifteen pounds during our six-day medical trip to Seattle earlier this year. I'm now up 20 pounds and I feel like I'm getting too heavy. I've lost so much muscle mass; shouldn't I weigh less? Also, my waist is larger than it's been in many years. When I tried on a pair of pants that I've worn for over 10 years, they were too small. This presents a dilemma for me. The medical people tell me not to lose weight, and, in fact the dietician that specializes in working with ALS patients told me that I should be eating 2850 calories a day—more than I ate pre-ALS. Because I'm inactive, that high of a caloric intake didn't make any sense. But should I now be packing on more weight? Extra weight makes it harder for me to stand, not that I stand all that much.

Plus, I'm having problems with pressure sores, or as they are often called, bedsores. I've cut back to ~1,500 calories a day, but am still slowly gaining weight. Does that mean my metabolism has slowed down?

If hypermetabolism means a more rapid decline that leads to an early death, then I'd hope for my metabolism to have slowed down. But, why would it have slowed? And if it has, will it stay at a slower rate? Even though I'd be considered over weight for my age if I didn't have ALS, more than one doctor has told me that it wouldn't hurt for me to weigh more. And no doctor, dietician, speech pathologist or other medical professional has told me to lose weight. Now that I have a PEG feeding tube, it seems that I could regain weight fast, if needed. One can of liquid food is 475 calories.

So, I'm going to try to lose ten to fifteen pounds. I mostly wear sweatpants, but I'd like to be able to wear the pants I used to wear. If a doctor tells me to put weight back on, I'll resort to the liquid food delivered via the PEG.

To quote from the study, "Our data are the first to indicate that hypermetabolism is a prognostic factor for ALS." Might measuring metabolism be a diagnostic tool in the future? To further quote, "Our primary finding is an increase in prevalence of hypermetabolism in patients with ALS compared with an age- and sex-matched control population. Hypermetabolic patients with ALS have a greater level of lower motor neuron involvement, faster rate of functional decline and shorter survival." Since one of the ways to slow down one's metabolism is to eat less, is the advice to not lose weight correct? Over time, eating less can slow metabolism. Or possibly, should drugs be used to slow metabolism in ALS patients? The unanswered question is, can slowing down one's metabolism slow ALS' progression? More research needs to be done, and the study be repeated to confirm that its findings are replicable. That seems like a good idea to me.

Gleason

5/7/18

One of the ALS news sources I follow suggested I watch the movie, *Gleason*, which chronicles the life of former NFL Football star Stephen Gleason, mostly after he was diagnosed with ALS. I easily found it on Google Movies, and was glad I watched it.

Unlike the movie *Augie*, which I didn't think was worth watching, I found *Gleason* worth every minute of my time. Also, unlike Augie the person, I found Stephen Gleason to be the kind of person I would like to have known before he was diagnosed with ALS, and I'd definitely like to know him now. Like Augie Nitro, Mr. Gleason started a nonprofit to help raise money for ALS sufferers. When watching *Augie*, I had the impression that his primary reason for starting his nonprofit was selfish. It's clear that Stephen Gleason's goals were altruistic. Both nonprofits, Augie's Quest and Team Gleason, are doing great things with the money that they are raising. However, Team Gleason funds go directly to help individuals with ALS—no middleman.

Stephen Gleason played football and NFL players are much more likely to develop ALS than those in the general population. Can head trauma play a role in causing ALS? Many football players also suffer the degenerative brain disease, Chronic Traumatic Encephalopathy (CTE). When a person suffers CTE, a protein called Tau forms clumps that slowly spread throughout the brain, killing healthy brain cells. Several studies now associate Tau not only with ALS, but Frontotemporal Dementia with Parkinsonism 17 (FTDP-17), Progressive Supranuclear Palsy (PSP), and others. Just like everything else associated with ALS, more research into brain trauma needs to be done.

Gleason is a good movie that helps portray what living with ALS is like for both the victim and the family. As in the movie, *Augie*, you will see that having enough money for full-time caregivers is a plus for longevity when living with ALS. Towards the end of *Gleason*, they admit this as well when a mechanical ventilator was placed in the trachea via a process called a tracheostomy. Team Gleason also lobbied for Congress to enact a law that has the potential to help everyone living with ALS. I encourage you to watch *Gleason*. You can find it on any Internet movie-streaming network.

Aphasia

5/12/18

The path to a diagnosis of ALS is usually not a straight path. Here is how it started for me.

When I started losing my ability to speak, Connie mentioned the word, aphasia. Never having heard the word before, and I asked her what it meant. She said it described the condition of not be able to express one's self or understand speech. Stroke victims often have aphasia. As my ability to talk became more and more hampered, we both wondered if I had suffered a stroke. When an MRI confirmed I had not had a stroke, we had to look elsewhere.

Diligent online research made us consider the possibility of a brain disorder called Primary Progressive Aphasia. But a second MRI and seeing a whole host of medical specialists in the Neurological Center at Virginia Mason Hospital gave us no answers. After I did okay on several cognitive tests, we began to think the preliminary diagnosis might be right. That was our first "Oh-my-God" moment. We had done enough research into Primary Progressive Aphasia to know it was devastating, early onset dementia. Nothing was scarier for us than me ending up in a vegetative state and wasting away to death. Our research also showed that Primary Progressive Aphasia often moves rapidly, and the victim quickly loses all abilities to understand both the verbal and written word. That scared us to no end.

Because we thought that I had a rapidly progressing dementia, early in 2015 we planned a road trip to see relatives in Colorado. We invited my younger sister, Chelly, to join us on the ferry trip south and the drive from Washington State to Colorado. Looking back, we are extra glad Chelly joined us. We had such a good time—lots of laughter and good conversations. At that time Chelly's cancer was in remission, and none of us knew it would come back with vengeance. I'm so very grateful we spent time with her while she was healthy, and before we lost her to the ravages of cancer. It's a rare day when I don't think of Chelly and miss her. A piece of Connie's art drawn in her memory sits directly above my computer, and each time I look up, I see it.

On that road trip, the ferry docked in Bellingham on a Friday morning and we made a beeline for Virginia Mason Hospital in Seattle. I met with the neurologist while Connie and Chelly walked our dog, Bella, in Freeway Park. After the neurologist finished her examination, she asked me to sit down. She had a serious look on her face, and as she started talking, I could see a tear roll down her face. She said, "I'm pretty sure you have Primary Progressive Aphasia." She knew we'd already talked about how devastating the disease is, and that she was sorry to have to give me the bad news. It's funny. What I remember most about that visit was feeling sorry, not for myself, but for the young doctor who had to give bad news. This neurologist was not long out of her schooling, and I assumed had not been hardened to giving bad news to a patient. I respected her more for openly showing her emotions than I would a doctor who stoically talks to a patient as if he or she was just an inanimate object.

Now that I can no longer talk and haven't been able to for over two and a half years, what do you call me? If I couldn't see, you'd say I was "blind." If I couldn't hear, you'd say I was "deaf?" "Dumb" was the term to label a person couldn't talk, but that's no longer right, and seems insensitive. Does the word, "mute," work? The dictionary entry for "mute" lists "dumb" as one the meanings, and vice versa. I do not want to be called "dumb." So, what do you call my malady?

My loss of voice should actually be called, dysarthria, a condition caused by the weakening of throat and speech muscles. Aphasia is the loss of language due to a brain disorder or stroke. My voice loss is caused by the loss of motor neurons located in the brain and spinal column. Exercising speech muscles in speech therapy can treat dysarthria, much like physical therapy strengthens other muscles. But no amount of speech therapy is effective with ALS dysarthria.

When I started to lose my voice, we all thought aphasia was the cause. Connie and I now know that was wrong. Besides "speechless" and maybe "mute," we still don't know what to call my malady. I call it a pain in the rear and many other not-so-nice things, and know it's not much fun. It sure can be isolating.

I'm not going to get depressed just because I can't talk. Though I often feel isolated, even in a room full of people, I'm going to stay upbeat. Sometimes conversations move along faster than I can type into my phone app, and other times, what I've already typed is no longer relevant. I just laugh at my inability to type as fast as teens do as I delete what I've typed and wanted to say. I'm not going to let this handicap, or any handicap get me down.

The path is not always straight. I'll soon tell you about my next diversion: Acromegaly.

Acromegaly

5/14/18

In late 2013 or early 2014 I noticed my voice would start cracking after a long day of work. At 61 years of age my voice would suddenly break as if I was once again entering puberty. I ignored it. I was working hard physical labor ten or more hours a day, six days a week, building a large house on a remote island in Southeast Alaska. When you build on a remote island with no roads, everything must be unloaded from a boat by hand, and in this case, moved up hill the length of a football field to the building site. Building in a remote area is several times harder than building on the road system. I came home each night totally exhausted—not a surprise. At the time my voice breaking was easily overlooked. After a good night's sleep, I'd wake up ready to hit it again, and my voice would be back to normal.

In August of 2014 the house was to a point that we could head out for a three-week European vacation. As we were about to board the plane my wife, Connie, commented that my voice sounded like I had suffered a stroke. I assured her I hadn't, but I had to face my months-long voice problems. Throughout our lovely holiday in Italy and France, the decline of my voice suddenly seemed to be on a fast track. I'd have to seek medical attention when we got home.

In September I saw Dr. Hunter, my primary physician and an internist, and as expected, he referred me to see a neurologist. Since we live in a small isolated town in Alaska with limited medical resources, it meant a trip to Virginia Mason Hospital in Seattle.

Over the next few months, I had two MRI's, countless blood tests, and two wrong guesses as to why I was losing my voice. In May of 2015 I saw neurologist Dr. Elliott for an Electromyography (EMG) test to see if I had ALS. The test came back negative, but Dr. Elliott took one look at my face and he asked, "Have you been tested for Acromegaly?" When I said no, he ordered blood tests to check my human growth hormone (HGH) and a hormone called Insulin–like growth factor one (IGF1).

At home, we went straight to Google to look up Acromegaly. It is a rare disorder where the body produces too much growth hormone. The excess HGH is usually caused by the growth of a benign tumor on the pituitary gland located at the base of the brain. The pituitary gland is often called the "Master Gland," because it controls the other glands in the body. The growth of a tumor on the pituitary can cause many of the body's fifty some hormones to be out of balance. The tumor can also grow large enough that it presses on the optic nerve causing blindness. Several famous people have had Acromegaly, the most notable being Andre the Giant.

Dr. Elliott guessed right. My HGH numbers were about twice as high as they should have been. And, the IGF1 was also high at 649, when it should be no more than 279. Dr. Elliott then referred me to see an endocrinologist at Virginia Mason. More blood tests and a third MRI confirmed that I did have a garbanzo bean–sized tumor growing on my pituitary gland.

As my voice continued to disappear, I was sent to see neurosurgeon, Dr. Farrokhi at Virginia Mason. Dr. Farrokhi suggested transsphenoidal surgery where an endoscope is used to reach the tumor at the base of the brain by going through the nose and sphenoid sinus. It's tricky surgery for several reasons. For one an ear, nose and throat (ENT) surgeon must access the base of the brain for the neurosurgeon. That requires cutting through a bone in the sinuses and then cutting through the skull just below the pituitary gland. The neurosurgeon then, has to be careful to not nick the optic nerve or cut the carotid artery, both of which sit next to the pituitary. If the optic nerve is nicked, you will go blind, and if the carotid artery is cut, there is a good chance of bleeding to death. Needless to say, you want a very experienced surgeon and both Connie and I felt good about Dr. Farrokhi's ability to perform this delicate operation.

In researching if Acromegaly could be the reason I was losing my voice, Dr. Farrokhi found that in rare Acromegaly cases soft tissue growth could cause loss of voice. So we all hoped my voice would come back after the surgery.

When my tongue started growing, Dr. Farrokhi was concerned that the anesthesiologist wouldn't be able to properly intubate me for surgery. To get my growth hormone lowered and hopefully shrink my tongue, my endocrinologist prescribed a month of the drug octreotide to be self-injected three times a day. I would do these injections at home under the supervision of Dr. Hunter. Just before I started the octreotide injections, Dr. Hunter asked to look at my tongue. I opened my mouth and tried, unsuccessfully, to stick out my tongue. He jumped back, and with a very surprised look on his face said, "Oh my, that's a big tongue." I'll never forget his reaction that day.

I have a phobia of needles, and since I'd never given myself an injection, we knew we'd need some training. Fortunately, a friend, who at the time was the training nurse at our local hospital, helped me face my fears and taught me the proper way to do the injections.

In August of 2015, I started the injections. I found the injections to be easier than I thought, but not the endless diarrhea and nausea side effects from the octreotide. Some get used to the octreotide, but I never did. The month of octreotide injections was the sickest I've ever been in my life. I switched to a time-release injection called a depot injection of Sandostatin, which would last a month. I was as sick as ever after that shot for the first three weeks.

The endocrinologist wanted to keep me on Sandostatin for a few months, but even though the drugs had made me sick, my tongue had shrunk and, I could go ahead with the surgery. By this time my voice had become nothing more than a whisper.

In early October Dr. Farrokhi had a much larger medical team than I expected. An ENT surgeon, another neurosurgeon, two anesthesiologists and whole host of surgical nurses spent five hours removing the tumor. After the surgery I was sent to the critical care unit for a day and a half, then two more days of recovering in a normal room. I think it was the day after the surgery when Dr. Farrokhi told me that he was confident that they removed the entire tumor, and said it looked old and was very fibrous.

An old tumor explained a great deal to me. In my early twenty's my hands and head grew. My hands grew from wearing large gloves to XX-large and my head grew to the point I need an extra-large hat. Then in my mid-forties my feet grew from a size 10 to size 12. In my 60s, along with the tongue growth, my jaw grew. I noticed that teeth I once had to force floss between became easier to floss. More disturbing, though, was a growth on my jaws called Gum Tori. This growth effected both my upper and lower jaw but was mostly on my lower left jaw. I now have a hard ridge of bone just below the gum line.

Here's a bit more about the transsphenoidal surgery. I expected a lot of pain post-surgery, but had almost no pain. While recuperating in the critical care unit a nurse gave me a pain pill and told me I should take it to stay ahead of the pain curve. I said I wasn't in any major pain, but I'd take the pill, and if I had any pain in the future, I'd let her know. I took that one pain pill and two Tylenol. My pain was not bad enough to require any meds. Also, I had none of the predicted bruising or swelling on my face.

Since the nasal packing needed to be removed a week after surgery and there was a potential of cerebrospinal fluid leak (CSF) from the brain, we stayed at a hotel owned by Virginia Mason Hospital directly across the street. It was a good decision.

Upon discharge I was given a prescription of Amoxicillin, an antibiotic, to take for a couple of weeks. Two days after being discharged and six days post-surgery, I got a rash in my groin, back and stomach, and was itching over most of my body. At the emergency room, I was told to stop taking the Amoxicillin, to take a couple of Benadryl pills, and to put Benadryl cream on the rash.

A week post-surgery the nasal packing was removed and there had been no CSF leaking. Even though the rash and the itching were getting worse by the minute, we were scheduled to go home the next day. Later that evening everything changed.

I'd been sleeping on and off, and around 8:00 p.m., I got up from bed to use the restroom, and I passed out. Connie later told me I sort of slid down the wall and landed flat on the floor. Connie called 911, and the next thing I knew several EMT's and a paramedic had lifted me back onto the bed and was taking my vitals. Then I was taken to the emergency room right across the street.

Once in the ER a blood pressure monitor showed my BP to be 40/20. An IV was started, and a finger blood oxygen monitor showed my oxygen level was dangerously low. When a nurse started to put the tubes of an oxygen cannula into my nostrils, Connie started to warn her of my recent surgery. The nurse said, "This man is dying, and we are trying to save his life." Connie stood her ground and said, "You need to know he had trans-sphenoidal surgery a week ago and what you are doing could cause a CSF leak." The somewhat overly excited nurse thanked Connie and the attending ER doctor assured both the nurse and Connie that the oxygen should be okay. To be sure he ordered a CT scan of my head, and all looked fine.

Four or five hours later, I was stabilized enough to be transferred to the critical care unit, where I spent the next four days. Then it was three more days in a normal room while I continued to recover. The allergic reaction to the Amoxicillin had caused a malady called erythema multiforme. The erythema multiforme rash covered every inch of my body with the worst rash that you can imagine. I looked like a boiled lobster, with almost my whole body turning fire engine red. The rash extended into my mouth and I was told it was likely that the rash also covered the inside of my intestines. The attending dermatologist told me that it was the worst case of erythema multiforme that he'd ever seen. Because the rash was so bad I think every medical student at Virginia Mason came to visit me. They all wanted to see what a bad reaction to a drug could look like, and I think their teaching doctors also wanted to see. I had become an interesting case study.

Though I had eluded pain from the transsphenoidal surgery, the itching and pain from the erythema multiforme made up for it. It took me several months to get over the erythema multiforme, and every inch of skin peeled off my body three times. Allergic reactions to antibiotics are serious. Though I had never reacted to any form of penicillin before, the Amoxicillin nearly killed me. If we hadn't been right across the street from the ER, I might not be here today.

The surgery to remove the tumor worked well. All my blood work over the ensuing two years showed normal numbers. An MRI one year after the surgery looked like the tumor might be growing back, but the radiologist and Dr. Farrokhi said it was scar tissue from the surgery.

At the end of 2015, I lost my voice completely. The loss of my ability to talk was not related to the Acromegaly. By the end of 2016, the neurologists assumed that I have Bulbar Onset ALS. As I write this in May of 2018, I'm confined to a wheelchair and have little doubt that I have Amyotrophic Lateral Sclerosis. My experience with Acromegaly was just a bump in the road on my journey living with ALS.

Dreams

5/16/18

We all have bizarre dreams from time to time. I sure do. This dream was so strange and bizarre that two months later I still remember it. In that dream, my wife Connie was laying vinyl tile on a big field of beautifully manicured green grass. By the time I walked up to her, she had already covered about an acre of the grass with a gawd-awful putrid gray and brown tile. I told her, "The adhesive is not going to stick to the grass. You need to put down a layer of gravel first." That's when I awoke—laughing at that whacky dream.

During my whole adult life I've solved hundreds of real problems in my dreams. The last house I built before ALS forced me into retirement had many tricky problems. It sits on a remote island off Sitka, so everything had to be moved by boat. I often solved material delivery logistic problems in my dreams. One of the biggest challenges was how to lift several heavy beams into place without a forklift or crane. The top-most beam, weighing over 700 pounds and measuring thirty feet long, forms the ridge of the house. It needed to be lifted over thirty feet off the ground. The beam lifting solution came to me in a dream, and it worked so well the owner, one helper and I had it in place in under an hour and a half. My dreams can be helpful as well as nonsensical.

And there are the "somewhere in-between" dreams. After watching a documentary about three young British men who drove across the Sahara Desert in 1959, I dreamed I was a passenger on a bus driving the length of the Sahara. I and several other men on the bus were talking about life and death. One particularly bitter old man dominated the conversation by endlessly criticizing the scenery, the bumpy road and saying everything about his life sucked. I jumped in and reminded him that much of life is what we make of it—exception: if we are cast into war zones or extreme poverty. If we have enough to eat, clothing and shelter, then much of the rest is up to us. We also choose how we want to face adversity. If we choose to be bitter and negative, we will be unhappy. Even when faced with a devastating disease like ALS, we can choose to be upbeat and happy. I reminded the negative man that we are the ones who can choose how we look at life and face our inevitable deaths.

When I awoke, it took me the longest time to figure out who the negative man was. He was someone from my past, but who? I finally remembered. It was the most negative man I've met in my life, and one whom I fortunately, encountered only briefly. His last name was Pontius, [pronounced like Pontius Pilate from the Bible, but no connection] but most people in Ketchikan called him, Pain-in-the ass. I'm sure he had a first name, but no one I knew used it. To his face he was Pontius; behind his back we all used the name that better suited him.

I first met Pontius when I worked for Ketchikan Public Utilities (KPU). He had been sentenced by a judge to do public service work at KPU for some small offence. During his first few days, I learned he had been in the Teamsters Union and had driven a truck during the construction of the Alaska Pipeline. After pipeline completion he drove freight to the oilfields on the Haul Road. He appeared to have a decent retirement because he drove a large ¾ ton truck with a big camper on the back where he lived. Every so often he'd take off on the ferry, but he always seemed to gravitate back to Ketchikan. Maybe the abundance of rain in Ketchikan and Southeast Alaska suited his ever-present grumpy mood.

Pontius was also a know-it-all. Within minutes of entering the Bailey Powerhouse, he was telling everyone how to do their jobs and criticizing everything he saw. Some hardworking guys who had been working for KPU for 25 to 30 years wanted to punch him in the nose. Because I only checked in and out of work at Bailey before working at other powerhouses, I missed most of his constant tirade of things that were wrong with the world. He was also a nonstop talker, but I don't think anything nice ever came out of his mouth. He would never greet anyone with a "Hi, how are you doing." Or say, "Goodbye, see you later."

After his public service work, I'd see him around town from time to time. If his truck was parked outside one store, I'd drive to another. When I saw him talking to people on the street, I immediately felt sorry for them. Once I saw his somewhat opposing figure standing over a poor woman whose hands were full of grocery bags, with two young kids in tow. He blocked her way, and forced her to listen to his negative rant, never offering to help or consider her needs.

My favorite Pontius story: Our son Zach, had a summer job for the US Forest Service as an onboard naturalist. Since he was headquartered in Juneau, we only saw him when he happened to pass through Ketchikan. He had a couple hour layover while the ferry unloaded and loaded, so Connie and I went to see him. As we approached the ferry terminal I saw Pontius' truck parked in one of the waiting lines to get on the ferry. The last thing I wanted was a Pontius encounter. Zach, in his sharp looking Forest Service uniform, walked handsomely off the ferry. Pontius made straight for the uniform, and, as expected, immediately started puking out an endless stream of how bad the Forest Service was, and how he'd fix it, if he were in charge. Zach let Pontius blather on for a few minutes, and then said something like this, "As an American I encourage you to express your 1st Amendment right to say what you want. You make some good points that I think you should share with the management of the Forest Service." Pontius appeared to be eating it up, but then Zach said, "I see you are about to drive onto the ferry. I'll tell you what, why don't you look me up once on board and I'll help you write a letter to the head of the Forest Service, and you can copy that letter to your representatives. I'm studying creative writing in college and between you and me, I think we can write one heck of a good letter." I was so proud of Zach, not only for putting up with Pontieus, but for being the first and only person I ever saw shut him up. Pontius walked away without saying another word, and didn't take Zach up on his offer. Pontius didn't want to change the world positively; he just wanted to make it miserable. Zach's offer to help him wasn't what he wanted at all. That didn't fit into his perhaps subconscious goal of infecting others with his wretched views of life.

I assume Pontius died a miserable death—that of a lonely, bitter man. He was a chain smoker and likely a heavy drinker. During the few years he was in Ketchikan, his raspy voice and persistent cough confirmed a long-term smoking habit. Looking back, I feel sorry for Pontieus. His grumpy negative personality drove away friends and family. As the saying goes, "We dig our own grave." I want to dig a grave full of happiness and love.

My Pontius dream was a reminder that negativity is the fertilizer of unhappiness. He was the most negative man I've ever met. As my ALS progresses, it would be easy to dwell on what I've lost, and not focus on all the positive things I have in my life. Positive things, like a ton of happy memories, and my family.

Life is good. I take that back. Life is GREAT.

Snake Oil

5/19/18

In the mid '60s, when I was about ten years old, my father purchased an old mercantile store in the small town of Sedalia, Colorado. At one time that mercantile sold everything—groceries, shoes, hardware, and farm equipment—even Dodge vehicles. The summer he purchased the store, we cleaned decades of dirt and grime from inside the large old stone building to ready it for opening as a small convenience grocery store. In the storage room I was fascinated by the wood framed bins that ran the length of the back wall just above a long workbench. The wall was about thirty feet long, with a 15-foot-high ceiling. An old, very dirty wood ladder that ran on a track like you sometimes see in old libraries gave access the high bins. What was inside the bins was even more fascinating than the bins themselves. They contained everything—bolts, nails, and over the counter medicines from days gone by.

That was my introduction to Snake Oil. You name it, there were bottles or small boxes of cures for everything you could dream up. Some bottles were small enough to fit in a breast pocket and some were as large as quart or more. Some of the bottles were clear, some blue, some green and some were brown. Some bottles had a liquid in them, some a powder and some had pills. Most had printed labels on them, and those labels were fascinating to read, even for a ten-year-old boy. Some of the labels claimed to be the cure for lumbago, some for a cold, some for rheumatism, and if I remember right, even cancer. I didn't know it at the time, but looking back, many of those questionable "medications" probably hadn't been legal to sell since around the time of the First World War. Being a young kid, I didn't fully appreciate I was seeing and holding a part of history each time I picked up one of the bottles to wipe away the years of accumulated dust.

Looking back at the old snake oil medicines, we wonder how people could be so gullible. I also wonder if I'm buying into the hype of snake oil each time I put a few drops of Cannabidiol (CBD) oil in my mouth? Is the CBD oil going to cure my ALS? The answer is, a very firm no. But maybe it will slow the progression of the disease? Despite some studies saying that CBD shows promise for ALS patients, I still wonder. It doesn't seem to be hurting me, so I'll keep using the very expensive CBD oil.

Some people will tell you that becoming a vegan has helped them with their ALS, or the other extreme, the ketogenic diet. Who is right? I think the old saying, "One man's meat is another man's poison," might apply here. Everyone's ALS is different, and everyone's body is different. Therefore, what works for one person might not work for the next. The answer to what works and what doesn't work calls to mind the quote I like so much; "It's more complicated than you think." The human body is a very complex biological machine. So, what's effective for you may not be effective for me. And some things are just pure snake oil, and won't work for anyone.

In today's Internet world there seems to be more snake oil salesmen than ever. Less than 30 seconds after I posted an ALS essay on Facebook last week, a comment showed up on my post for an ALS cure. Wanting a cure won't produce one. Another day another Facebook Friend had her account hacked. The hacker made me think her Messenger account was offering up to $200,000.00 in government grants that I didn't have to pay back. Nice, but again, not true. Every couple of weeks one of the ALS sites that I follow posts a false miracle cure that the site moderator quickly takes down. One ALS nonprofit also appears a bit shady, and borders on snake oil with the promises they promote on their site.

So, why do we people sometimes fall for these cure-all schemes? Financial desperation? We need money to cover the expenses due to our illness. Even though something deep inside tells us two hundred grand with no strings attached is too good to be true, we take the bait. Or, we want a cure so much we'll try anything. I don't blame anyone for falling for these schemes. It's human nature to be trusting, and lowlife snake oil salesmen take advantage of that. I hope the lowlife scum that profit from others' misfortunes will have karma bite them in the rear. There are few things lower than snake oil salesman or saleswomen who knowingly push false hopes. I'm vindictive enough to wish them true karma. They deserve it.

Power Wheelchair Saga

5/22/18

Six weeks ago, today, we started the process to obtain an electric, or as some call them, a power-wheelchair. We had been warned that the process could be complicated and would take three or more months, especially, since we live in a small remote Alaska town. Medicare has some strict rules when it comes to paying for a chair. At first, I thought, "Oh man, more rules." Now I understand that Medicare wants to make sure that every chair they help pay for is the right chair for the person's needs.

For inside mobility I don't need a power-wheelchair—yet. But my manual chair limits where I can go outside the house. An electric wheelchair would let me join Connie and Bella on walks in the park, and help fight off cabin fever that will eventually plague me. In the house I hang out on one floor in bed, at the dining table, or at my computer. I also dip into the restroom and the kitchen—a fairly boring existence, if I can't add in some outdoor time.

We will soon be heading to Virginia Mason Hospital in Seattle where I can be properly measured and evaluated for the power chair, and attend a Combined Wheelchair Clinic. At a local wheelchair supply company I will meet with a Physiatrist [per Google, "A physiatrist is a medical doctor or doctor of osteopathic medicine who specializes in Physical Medicine and Rehabilitation (also called PM&R physicians). Physiatrists diagnose and treat both acute pain and chronic pain and specialize in a wide variety of nonsurgical treatments for the musculoskeletal system."], an Occupational Therapist (OT) and an Assisted Technology Professional (APT). The Physiatrist will assess my past medical history, current needs, and try to predict my future needs. The OT will assess my physical and functional abilities. And last, the APT will work with the team to determine the best wheelchair for my needs. They will take into considerations, what kind of mobility I will need in the house and outdoors. I will be sure they know I want to be able to use the chair on the handicapped-accessible gravel trails, like the main trail in the Sitka Historical National Park, or, the Muskeg Loop Trail. After all this consultation, I'll try a power chair for the first time, and be measured, so that a chair can be custom built from standard components for me. It's a royal hassle to get the chair, but since Medicare will only pay for a new wheelchair every five years, it is worth doing it right.

A power wheelchair means we will need to get a handicapped-accessible van. Connie and I are total neophytes when it comes to knowing what van to buy. We are both staggered by sticker shock. New vans can cost over $70,000, and a decent low-end van is still going to cost over $30,000.00. We didn't pay much over that for our first house in 1977. By the time you factor in the price of two airline tickets to Seattle, a hotel, rental car, medical expenses that Medicare and my insurance won't pay, and the van, a power-wheelchair will end up costing us between $40-50,000.00. Who knew that being handicapped was so expensive? I didn't.

Sadly, the money we saved for retirement will get eaten up for medical expenses. We had hoped to travel, and I had aspirations of combining travel with volunteer work like many of our friends do. Now, even to enjoy the outdoors in my own back yard will take a big bite out of savings. It's hard not to get a bit depressed by that. But I'm not going to let the ALS Monster depress me as it chips away at the person I had hoped to be at this age.

How Rude!

5/3/2018

Medicare requires that I see either my primary care doctor or my pulmonologist every three months before they will let me order new supplies for my BIPAP machine, necessary for me to breath when I sleep. Connie and I also wanted to fill in Dr. Hunter in on our upcoming trip to Seattle to get measured for a power wheelchair. As my primary care and internist, he will become an important part of the Medicare equation for future assessments and possible accessories I might need for the chair. It was a double important visit to see Dr. Hunter.

On our drive into Sitka Community Hospital, two different teenage drivers were driving the wrong way, making it hard for Connie to enter the parking lot. After parking and placing the handicap parking decal on the rearview mirror, Connie got my wheelchair from the truck and I moved into it. Connie walked around me, opened the clinic door, and just as I was about to roll myself through, a young man in his mid-thirties stepped in front of me, literally turning sideways to fit between my wheelchair and the door. How rude! Twice—the guy jumping in front of me, and the teens driving the wrong way.

My faith in humanity was soon restored. After entering the doctor's office, Elaine, a woman I used to work with at Sheldon Jackson College, came over and gave me a big hug. She held my hand for a long time, and said so many nice things about me I started to turn red. Then when Dr. Hunter's young, friendly and caring nurse came to get me, even more of my faith was restored. The icing on the cake was the visit with Dr. Hunter, who was nice, friendly and compassionate as ever. I am so lucky to have a good primary care doctor here in Sitka.

There will always be a few jerks, but most people are good at heart. My visit to the doctor's office fortified my faith in people, shortly after it had been knocked down.

Santa

December 12, 2016

Although tenuously connected to ALS and out of order, this essay has been included.

ALS not only steals physical abilities, but it steals things we enjoy doing. Some of my most satisfying memories are of volunteering for various nonprofits. ALS has mostly stolen that from me, but it can never rob me of the memories that make life worth living.

A post on Facebook got me thinking about the 20-plus years I played Santa and how much fun it was. During that time babies have wet their pants and spit up on me while I held them in my lap, and lots of little children have cried in fear. It was fun to calm them down so they could enjoy their visit with Santa. I could never write all my stories of what kids want for Christmas.

I've never much liked my photo being taken, but as Santa, I was front and center on hundreds of family Christmas cards. One preschool always scheduled the timing of Santa for the Saturday after Thanksgiving and even offered a Christmas card photo service with a child or the full family. I often laughed thinking about my photo being proudly displayed all over the nation, as many of the families and children that came for the photos with Santa where Coast Guard families from all over the USA. I loved it, not because I wanted to be seen in photos, but because I could be a small part of helping make precious family memories.

I have always had a long bushy beard, so I never needed a fake beard to play Santa. For the first 10 years I had to dye my brown beard white. Each year I needed less and less dye, and the last 10 years my beard was plenty white to pass as the official Santa. More than one kid told me they knew I was the real Santa because I had a real beard. I even loved it when the little kids pulled my beard "just to be sure." Most times, my wife Connie would dress up as an elf or Mrs. Claus and come with me. During our first trip to Europe while visiting Germany, she bought a pair of authentic leather lederhosen to wear to look more like an elf.

I loved playing Santa, and especially loved the little kids. And, oh, the things they'd ask for! One very cute three-year-old true Alaskan girl asked me for a quad (an ATV four-wheeler). She even had the model number, and as she walked away she looked over her shoulder and added, "Oh, and don't forget the snow plow for the front of the quad." Many little boys asked for hunting rifles and typical little boy's toys. Not surprising, the most popular item for little girls was dolls, with the American Girl doll being number one, followed closely by Barbie. Each year I would try to be "up" on the latest toys, but I was never prepared for the details the little girls would go into when it came to what outfit Barbie or some other doll needed. I always took comfort, as I'd watch parents take mental notes about what their child wanted, and if I thought the parent didn't hear, I would try to repeat the child's words.

One of the best ways to get a shy child to open up was to start teasing them. For shy little girls, I'd say something like, "You want a dump truck and maybe a big tractor, don't you?" If they shook their heads "No," I'd say, "Oh a monster truck, then?" After my 3rd or 4th fake guess they would start rattling off what they wanted. Sometimes it was hard to get a child to give up his or her turn with me. Those who came back through the line, or on a different day, to test me on what they wanted were really tough. I'd do my best to trick them into thinking I knew, but I needed them to retell me.

Though mostly a lot of fun, there were sad times, too. It broke my heart when I could tell that the family had limited money and there was no way the child was going to get he or she wanted. Or one time when at the Woman's shelter a kid said, "I just want my Dad back." Once a little boy said he didn't want his daddy to hit his mommy anymore. The hardest was when a little three-year-old girl asked me for a new little brother. Her little friend told me her little brother had just died, and as I looked over at the little girl's parents I could see the pain in their faces as they nodded, "Yes." I had tears in my eyes when I remembered holding their newborn baby the previous year. He was only a few days old, and I remembered how extra cute he was. There was nothing I could say to comfort the little girl as I hugged her. I'm tearing up just recalling how sad that was for me, but most especially for the little girl's parents. I truly can't think of a deeper pain than to lose a little baby. As much as I hate ALS, I'll take it one hundred times over if I could keep a parent from suffering the pain of losing a child, most especially a baby.

I've always had a very soft spot for babies, especially little baby girls. As Santa I got to hold many, many newborns and have had more than one parent tell me that I was the first stranger ever to hold their child. One year a baby boy just a few weeks old was crying and crying, and his mother could do nothing to comfort him. Since no other children were waiting, I asked the mother if I could hold her baby for a while. As I lifted the little tyke to my shoulder and started walking him around the room, he stopped crying and was soon fast asleep. The mother joked that I was hired knowing how little sleep new mothers get. I'm guessing she was only half joking. For those few minutes walking that newborn I basked in the warm feeling only possible knowing you have comforted a child.

I still have my Santa suit, but should give it to the next generation Santa. Maybe Connie should give her elf costume away, too. Christmas has always been about the joy that holiday brings to children. I'm very happy and cherish all my memories of my Santa years. No more Santa; ALS robbed me of that, as well.

Lots of little children are excited about the idea of seeing Santa, but when the time comes for them to sit on Santa's lap, it's another story. And many children are outright scared of Santa. That was always okay with me. I always did my best to show them I wasn't so scary, but always told them it was okay to be afraid. When a parent has their mind set on getting a photo of their child or children with Santa, the fright issue can become a real problem. Most parents will try to comfort the child, but the technique that I always liked best was when the braver sibling would hold the hand of the less brave sibling. Together they would sit on my lap and tell me what they wanted. Another technique that worked well was when the mother would sit on my lap and the child in their mother's lap. Dozens of mothers have sat on my lap while the photographer is clicking away and the child is talking to me, or more often, to me via their mother. Only once did I mind using that technique. A father, very likely pushing the 300-hundred-pound mark on the scale, decided to sit in my lap while holding his child. I no longer remember a single thing about the child, but I sure remember the day that monster man sat in my lap.

Often kids way beyond believing in Santa would come sit on my lap, or a group of giggling girls would more or less dare their friends to sit in Santa's lap, and one by one, would do so. I never enjoyed that much because it put me in a rather weird position—not wanting to be some sort of pervert, but also not wanting to offend or hurt the child. Tons of women have come to sit in Santa's lap and tell me what they want—everything from a husband to a sports car. One of Connie's rather boisterous coworkers sat on my lap and announced for all to hear that she wanted a red Ferrari. I promised her she'd get one, and, with Connie's help, she did, albeit, a red Ferrari Matchbook car. One year three young women in their 20s took turns sitting on my lap, and when it came time for the last lady, the other two, one on each side of me, kissed my cheeks. Then they told me this was going to be their Christmas card. It was a good thing Connie was there or she might have wondered why I had lipstick on my cheeks.

More than once kids or families would show up in their pajamas to have their photos taken with Santa. One family, dad, mom and three or four children were all dressed in matching pajamas. Dad, mom and the youngest child were fine being seen in public in their pajamas, but I could tell the teenage daughter wasn't at all amused. Lots and lots of kids and families came dressed in their Sunday best to have their photos taken. I especially liked seeing the little boys all dressed in full three-piece suits—that's about as cute as anything you could ever imagine. One time three young extra cute sisters, aged from about three to eight, came all dressed in beautiful homemade green velvet dresses with big red sashes, white tights with extra shiny black patent leather shoes. Their father, a man about 50, worked construction around town. When visiting with a mutual friend of ours later, I said I was surprised that the father had such young daughters. The friend responded, "Just a few weeks ago, they adopted the girls." I was impressed. Here was a childless couple, both approaching 50, adopting and taking responsibility for three young sisters, thus keeping them in the same household. I was again impressed when the same well-behaved girls visited Santa the following Christmas. It was obvious that the girls were all well loved, and all had new homemade dresses.

Possibly one of my strangest and maybe most unique Santa experiences took place one warm spring day in Seattle just a few years ago. I had traveled to Seattle with a young woman named Zia who was working for a nonprofit to attend a Saturday morning breakfast meeting. After the meeting, Zia asked me to show her some of the tourist sites in Seattle because she hadn't spent much time there, and knew I had. After taking her to Pike Place Market, we skipped the Space Needle because of the long lines, and sat by the International Water Fountain in the park that was built for the 1962 World's Fair. The fountain sits inside a large concrete lined basin in the center of which is a large stainless steel half-sphere with about 20 nozzles that randomly shoot water to synchronized music. On hot days kids of all ages race in the water and play "chicken" with the shooting fountains seeing how close they can come without getting totally soaked. This day it wasn't warm enough to actually play in the water, but kids still ran around the slanted concrete walls that form the catch basin for the fountain. Soon, a boy of about six years of age came up to me and asked if I was Santa. I said I was and that I was in Seattle to enjoy some sunny weather because it was still way too cold at the North Pole. He then ran off, and I could see him talking to his mother on the other side of the fountain. He kept running around the fountain, talking to me, and then back to talk to his mother. Then, to my surprise I saw his mother shooing him towards me. He ran to me, asked if he could sit on my lap and tell me what he wanted for Christmas. Only because it was obvious that his mother could see what we were doing, I complied, and he sat on my lap for about five minutes. He told me his whole life story, plus what he wanted for Christmas, still a half a year away. After that he happily ran off. We quickly moseyed on, as the last thing I needed was more kids wanting to see Santa in the spring. Zia and I laughed about my Santa experience for the rest of our Seattle "tour;" the Fremont Troll sculpture, Ballard Locks and then to the park by Shilshole Bay Marina where we watched the sun set.

Having a big white beard has had more than the advantage of keeping my face warm. It has brought me many fun memories and I'm happy that I could be a very small part of the magic that makes Christmas a special time of year. ALS might have forced me into retirement, with 2013 being the last year I played Santa. But over the years that I did play Santa, not only did I make lots of good memories for Connie and me, we helped make good family memories for others. When I'm long gone, some Santa photo will trigger good memories. As ALS continues to steal abilities from me, knowing that the simple act of putting on a Santa suit brought joy to so many people. And, that brings joy to me, every day of the year, but most especially during the Christmas Season.

All photos were taken in 2002.

The Past, Present, Future and Death

June 2018

THE PAST

ALS is always fatal. It has a 100% death rate. There is no cure, and the leading cause of death in ALS patients is respiratory failure. Those words don't leave a lot of room for hope. And, without hope, why continue to fight? Why not just give in and give up? My answer: I'm going to do all I can to fight the ALS Monster as it continues to chip away at me, to stay happy, and make each day count.

I'm not happy about having ALS. But would I go back and change my history and wipe ALS off the slate? The answer is yes and no. Yes, because ALS has robbed, and will continue to rob, me of my abilities to do things, and the end game for the Monster is death. But, like most bad things in my past, I'd have to say no. Even if I could, I wouldn't change my past. I'll try to explain.

Religious people often feel like they become closer to their religion when their faith is tested. As they struggle to maintain their beliefs during a test, their faith often becomes stronger, making them better people. I'm not religious, but I feel elation when I win even a small victory against the ALS Monster. I've experienced what it is to ward off depression, bitterness, anger, frustration and many other negative emotions. There is a great satisfaction in doing that. I get happiness out of knowing that the ALS Monster hasn't won over my mind, and that it isn't giving me depression or bitterness.

Life is nothing but a series of experiences strung together that mold us into who we are. Additionally, there are forces like our DNA that we can't control. When our DNA, or some other outside force, gives us an adverse experience, it's up to us how we deal with it. I don't like ALS, but I'm also grateful for many of the experiences it has brought me. Some of the best people I have met are because of my ALS. As negative as ALS has been, it has also brought many rewards I wouldn't have experienced without it. I'm grateful for that.

The other night we were watching a documentary on extreme poverty in Nepal, one of the poorest countries on earth. The documentary showed how hard it is for people to feed their families to get enough to eat, afford shelter and all the things that we take for granted. As we watched, I typed into my phone for Connie to read, "I'd rather live in America with ALS, than to live with that kind of poverty." Life is a struggle living with ALS, but I'm lucky I was to be born into a middle-class life in an affluent country. Even the ALS Monster can't rob from me of where I was born, or the happy memories that Connie and I have made together.

PRESENT

I can no longer verbally speak, chewing and swallowing are difficult, my breathing is labored, my legs no longer function well enough to walk, and poor blood circulation in my legs causes them to swell daily. That's the short list of what the ALS Monster has taken from me, but I'm not going to focus on the negative.

I'm thankful that I have a loving wife and that we live in such a beautiful place. I'm thankful that we live in a nice house and that we can afford to eat good food. I'm especially thankful that my son and his family live so close by. And, I'm, for sure, thankful for our little dog, Bella. Each and every day she brings me such joy. In spite of ALS, I'm living a good life.

FUTURE

In order to look ahead, I need to look back. I started losing my voice in early 2014. Was that the start of my ALS? If so, that means I've been living with ALS for over four years. I wonder, though, if I was experiencing the start of ALS much sooner? A good exercise for ALS patients to keep their diaphragms strong is to blow up balloons. My diaphragm and even my lip muscles may have been getting weaker sooner than I thought. I recall having trouble blowing up a balloon for one of my grandsons maybe two years before I started losing my voice. Was that the start of my ALS? If so, then I'm at least five years into the ALS journey.

It doesn't really matter when my ALS started, except statistics say ALS kills most people in three to five years from onset. Am I already living on borrowed time? No one can answer that, because ALS treats every victim differently. In some it runs a very rapid course, and in others, it is slow. I, of course, hope I have a slower progressing ALS, and so far, it looks like I do.

Slow or not, ALS will keep marching on, and I'll need to make some major decisions. ALS's number one cause of death is respiratory failure, using a mechanical ventilator when the diaphragm muscle gets too weak to breathe naturally is the only way to extend life. If I was younger with young children, or had a brain like Stephen Hawking, I'd opt for the ventilator. But at my stage of life, the thought of lying around with a functioning brain unable to move haunts me. So - no ventilator. I currently use a BIPAP ventilator when sleeping, and I'm open to using a portable battery powered BIPAP later when I need a little assistance.

I already have a PEG feeding tube that I mostly use for liquids. In the future, I'll have to use it for all sustenance. I'm okay with that, too. I'll miss the taste of food, but when I have to, I'll use the PEG.

I'm currently able to bathe and dress myself, and can get myself on and off the toilet. Eventually I'll need help with all the above. That bugs me and giving up independence will be hard; I must accept what the future brings. I just hope it's a long way off, and that I have a chance to chronicle many more years of this journey.

I can't travel extensively or do the volunteer work I wanted to do in retirement, but when we get a handicapped-accessible van, maybe we can go on a road trip. It won't be easy, but travel enriches the soul, and helps keep the blues away.

I'd be lying if I said that I wasn't a bit apprehensive about the future, but I can't stop time. Fear of what's to come is often worse than the reality when it gets here. No one knows what waits around the next bend. Just as when Connie and I were doing a lot of caving, I'll keep sticking my head around the next bend and take it as it comes. I may not always like what I find, but I'm strong enough to deal with it.

DEATH

The ALS Monster will keep chipping away at me until my death. I'll be pleased to deprive it of the satisfaction it seems to get from watching its victims struggle. I'm not afraid of death per se. I have already experienced what it's like to struggle for air– very scary. Every day for about two years on this journey, I would choke badly enough that I'd struggle to breath, many times, coming close to passing out. That's frightening. Awaking from a sound sleep choking on my own saliva in a full panic – that's darn scary. Choking now only happens on rare occasions.

They say that cats have nine lives, and that must be the same with me. I'd have to think hard to count how many close scrapes with death I've had – a couple of long falls climbing; one, a sixty-foot un-roped fall into a crevasse on Mt. Rainer, should have killed me. Once I came close to drowning while cave diving. And when I was about five years old, I would have drowned if my best friend Jimmy's older sister hadn't pulled me from the bottom of a pond. And, my stepmother came close to beating me to death multiple times. I'm lucky to have overcome more odds than I should have.

The ALS Monster probably hopes this "cat" is nearing its ninth life, and is looking forward to winning. On many occasions I walked the razor's edge where the risk of death was staggeringly high. Once I dove in a cave to a depth of 266 feet, over twice the sports diving department limit. One

248

equipment failure, one miscalculation, or one physiology problem (like nitrogen narcosis or oxygen toxicity) would have lead to death. Another time I swam 800 feet though a tunnel and back 100 feet deep on an inspection dive. Before I started I knew I'd have an air reserve of 10% if all went well; any equipment failure would have meant death.

Any participant in extreme sports or other hazardous activities has two basic choices; deny the risk, or accept death as a strong possibility. I've always known that a mistake, equipment failure, or a physiological problem could lead to death, and have willingly continued with these activities; their rewards out-weighing the risk of death. I can't beat the odds of death, but I've tried to fully experience the journey.

Death is inevitable, and I, as have others, pushed the limits of that inevitability. Maybe that's why I'm not afraid of ALS's downward sloping road.

Acknowledgments

I want to thank my wife, Connie, for all her help putting together this book. She was always the first one to read my drafts and make suggestions.

I'd also like to thank two amazing people I met when I worked at Sheldon Jackson College; Charles and Blanche Iliff. It was Chuck and Blanche who introduced me to the awesome Dana Anderson. I could never have put this book together with out Dana's help editing my essays. Thank you, Dana.

September 2, 2018. Connie LaPerriere, wife of Marcel, Nate LaPerriere, middle son of Zach and Jenn, Blake LaPerriere, eldest son of Zach and Jenn, Marcel LaPerriere, Zach LaPerriere, son of Connie and Marcel, Jenn Lawlor, wife of Zach LaPerriere, and Dane (Lucky) LaPerriere, youngest son of Zach and Jenn. Bella, the dog, in front. Jenn Lawlor photo.

About the Author

Marcel started an apprenticeship as a machinist in High School. He completed that apprenticeship in Seattle for a machine tool rebuild company, and later ran a machine shop before starting his own company machining injection molds and other custom work. After moving to Alaska, he became a powerhouse mechanic, and in Sitka ran the maintenance department for Sheldon Jackson College until they closed. His last major commercial venture before ALS hastened his retirement was a construction company specializing in custom homes using local woods.

Marcel has always loved adventure and being outdoors. Initially, he climbed in Colorado and the Wyoming Tetons in high school, continuing in Washington and Canada. Sailing became his next adventure, one his wife and son could enjoy with him—they lived on a boat for over 25 years. Next, he started scuba diving and became a Dive Master, did some wreck diving and became certified as a cave diver. Both his wife and son joined him in caving. All three walked Alaska Forest Service units to map caves and protect them from damaging development. This led to a desire to protect the environment in support of which he wrote many letters, and was a board member and the President for a few years of the Sitka Conservation Society.

He and his wife enjoyed traveling to Europe, especially climbing Via Ferrate's in Italy and France. Watching his three grandsons grow has been one of the biggest highlights of his life, and they all enjoyed tales of his exploits.

ALS has changed his life, but he views it as just another adventure.

CPSIA information can be obtained
at www.ICGtesting.com
Printed in the USA
BVHW010138090119

537207BV00012BA/588/P